Discover St Davids

Pembrokeshire Publications

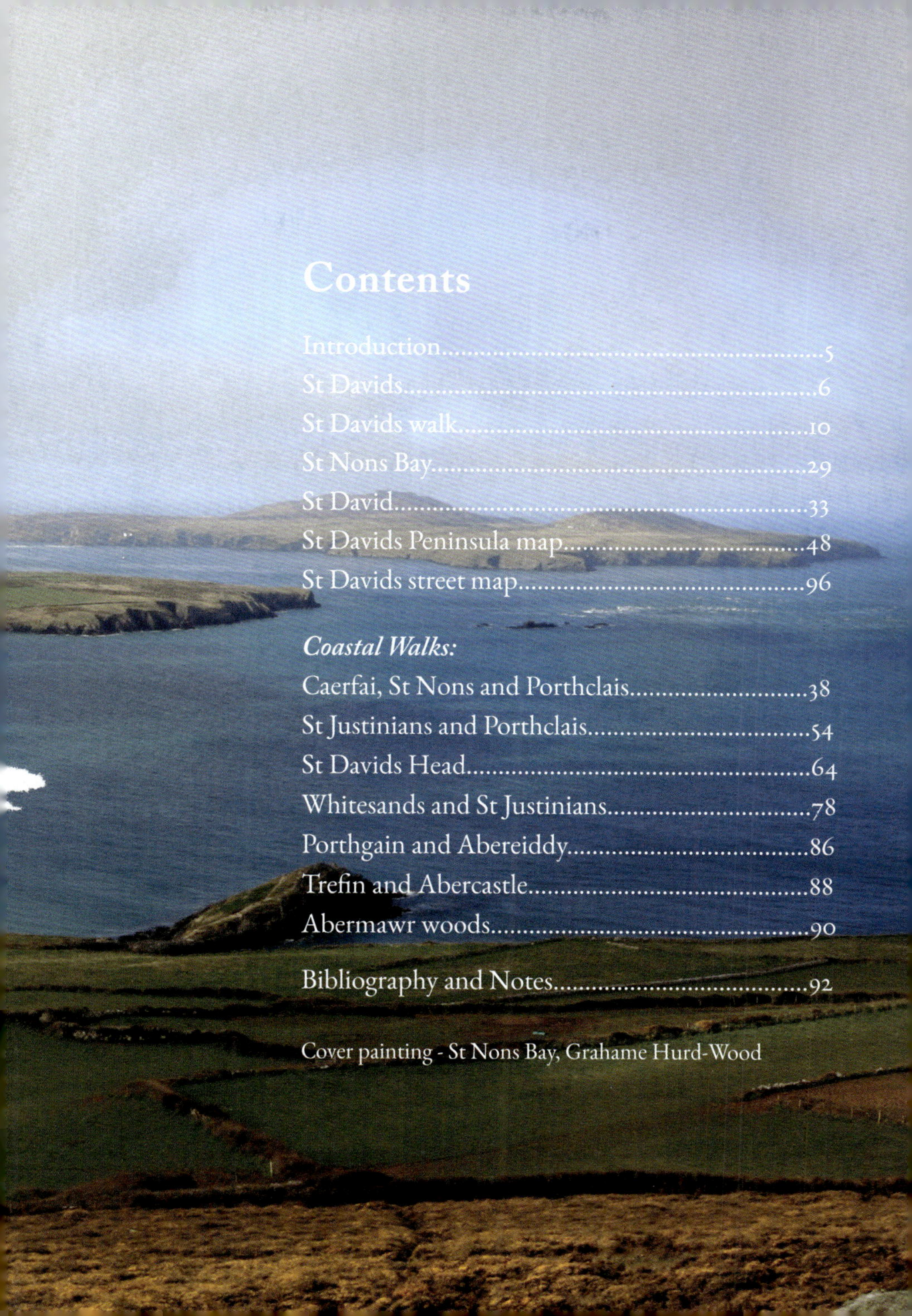

Contents

Cover painting - St Nons Bay, Grahame Hurd-Wood

Timeline

Mesolithic: 8,000 BC – 4,000 BC. Nomadic hunter-gathering and fishing, with rudimentary forms of cultivation in temporary settlements. Worked flint flakes found around the St Davids Peninsula, along with spear and arrow heads on Whitesands beach.

Neolithic: 4,000 BC – 2,500 BC. The birth of farming, with the domestication of animals and the creation of more settled communities. The development of communal, stone burial chambers.

Bronze Age: 2,500 BC – 700 BC. The first use of metals, initially copper and then bronze. The development of standing stones and stone circles. Communal burial chambers change to single chambers, mainly for the elite.

Iron Age: 700 BC – 70 AD. The processing of iron ore, producing more effective tools, farming implements and weapons. Widespread development of defensive hill and coastal promontory forts.

Romano British: 70 AD – 410 AD. Conquest of England and Wales by the Romans is completed by the end of the first century AD, although there is no evidence of Roman settlement on the peninsula. Large settlement of Irish on the peninsula from the fourth century AD.

Early Medieval: 410 AD – 1066 AD. The Age of the Saints, 400 to 600 AD, with the foundation of early Christian monasteries. The birth of David in the sixth century and the foundation of his monastery in the late sixth century. The monastery was subsequently attacked and raided thirteen times between 878 and 1091, mainly by Vikings.

Medieval: 1066 AD – 1536 AD. The Norman invasion of Britain begins. Visit by William the Conqueror to David's shrine in 1081. The first stone cathedral built in 1131. David canonized in 1133, promoting a huge increase in pilgrimage to his shrine. The Reformation begins in 1534, with the halt of pilgrimage and the Dissolution of the Monasteries.

Introduction

All the walks in this guide can be accessed by public transport from St Davids, mainly on the excellent Celtic Coaster which runs from the Easter school holidays to the end of September. Timetables are at pick-up points throughout the area and available at the Oriel y Parc Visitor Centre, St Davids.

The visitor centre, and major car park, is on the signposted road to Caerfai off the St Davids to Haverfordwest A487 road. The other large car park in St Davids is in the Merrivale Valley on the road to St Justinians, a closer walk to the cathedral close. There are smaller car parks on Quickwell Hill off Nun Street, above the cathedral close and in New Street by the supermarket. Postcodes are included through the guide where practical. The Ordnance Survey maps for all the walks and covering north Pembrokeshire are Explorer OL35 (1:25 000) and Landranger 157 (1:50 000). OL35 is more detailed for walking.

For walks further afield the Strumble Shuttle runs north along the coast from St Davids to Fishguard, and the Puffin Shuttle runs south along the coast from St Davids to Marloes. Both services are available throughout the year, with a limited service in the winter. Timetables are at pick-up points in St Davids and available at the visitor centre.

The Celtic Coaster route is: Visitor Centre car park, City Hall, St Nons (Drop-off point), Cathedral, Porthclais Harbour, St Justinians, Nun Street, Lleithyr, Whitesands Bay, Lleithyr, New Street, Visitor Centre car park.

Walking shoes or boots are highly recommended for the coast path, and any of the coastal and rural routes can be muddy in parts in wet weather. Please keep dogs on a lead on the coast path.

Oriel y Parc Gallery Visitor Centre and Landscape Gallery, St Davids SA62 6NW. Open seven days a week March to October 9.30am – 5pm. November to February 10am – 4pm. Tel. 01437 720392.

St Davids

It was around 540 AD that a tall, charismatic Celt and his followers lit their first fire of settlement beside the River Alun in the little valley of Glyn Rhosyn.

The smoke curving above the trees and jackdaws, an ancient rite of claim to land, was a transforming action; a skyward spiral into a village-city that lies at the spiritual heart of Wales.

St Davids Cathedral and the Bishop's Palace

For over 1,400 years the site St David chose for a monastic settlement has been a place of sanctity. It is one of the most ancient centres of Christian worship in Britain.

The layout of Britain's smallest city has not changed since medieval times, although its appearance has: 'I kept on fancying that snow had fallen,' the enthusiastic diarist and clergyman Francis Kilvert commented in the autumn of 1871, such was the extent of limewashing to the house walls and many roofs. The kilns at the nearby harbour of Porthclais provided a plentiful supply.

Other commentators were not so kind. Twenty years earlier the historians Jones and Freeman described St Davids as, 'something like a town, consisting chiefly of mean houses, a few of them thatched, all of course whitewashed, and built so irregularly as scarcely to deserve the appellation of a street . . . some have courtyards in the front, a few have gardens, but by far the majority have pigsties.'

They were, however, later to describe great improvements in the community's housing within the space of a few years; and of the cathedral close and the peninsula's natural beauty they were nothing if not enthusiastic.

The streets of St Davids radiate out from the Cross Square, as they have since medieval times. The square is named after the fourteenth-century preaching cross that lies at its centre, one of four that are said to have existed on the approaches to the gateways of the cathedral close.

The square was then a place of public gatherings and meetings, where travelling fairs provided entertainment and a twice-weekly market was held. Restored in the nineteenth century, the cross is said over the centuries to have inspired honesty in market dealings.

St David's first Post Office, in New Street, around 1890

The medieval cross on the Square

St Davids' first lifeboat, the Augusta, arrived in 1869 and was initially kept under tarpaulin on a carriage in the garden of what is now the Old Cross Hotel, and was horsedrawn to the sea, to whatever embarkation point was closest for a rescue.

Hollowed grooves at the base of the cross itself were made by ropes hauling the boat from the Old Cross before being tethered to horses.[1] The lifeboat was eventually housed on the coast at St Justinians.

The Memorial Gardens of the square commemorate the men of the parish who lost their lives in the two world wars. The flagpost was erected in 1912 as a memorial to the men who died when the St Davids lifeboat, the Gem, was lost in Ramsey Sound.

Much of the attractive patchwork of buildings that nestle around the square dates from before Kilvert's day, although the blacksmiths, milliners and gentlemen's outfitters of the nineteenth century have given way to a gentle bustle of cafes, restaurants, galleries, fashion and water-sport shops all within easy reach.

In the mid-nineteenth century travel 'abroad' by public transport was by horse and carriage, and a service departed from the square. It took up to three hours to travel the 'sixteen hills and sixteen miles' to Haverfordwest, with the men alighting at Solva and Newgale to walk up the hills. In 1869 the fare was 2/6 inside and 2/- outside.[2] Buses provided a service from 1915.

The streets running out from the square lead along ancient routes of trade and travel. South to the harbour of Porthclais runs Goat Street, formerly Ship Street, along which two nineteenth-century granary warehouses still stand. A little further on towards Porthclais, in Catherine

Street, is another fine granary.

The other streets run north to Fishguard along Nun Street, said to be named after St Non, the mother of St David, and east along the High Street to Haverfordwest. This is Britain's smallest city, with a population just under 2,000.

The top of the graceful sixteenth-century cathedral tower is visible from the square and The Pebbles, a name given to the cobbled stones with which the road was once partly paved, lead down to the walled, medieval Close.

New Street in the 1890's

St Davids

St Davids Walk

A walk through the centre of St Davids and the cathedral close with its lovely, medieval calm. There is an optional detour to the coast at St Nons to visit the ancient chapel and healing well of St David's reputed birthplace, in a beautiful setting overlooking the Atlantic.

Time: Two hours for the full route including St Nons Bay.

Distance: Two miles for the full route, half a mile for the shorter route.

Terrain: A moderate walk along streets and rural paths. Some short inclines.

Facilities: Pubs, restaurants, cafes, WC's.

Getting there: The car park opposite the visitor centre SA62 6NW, although the walk can be followed from any area of St Davids.

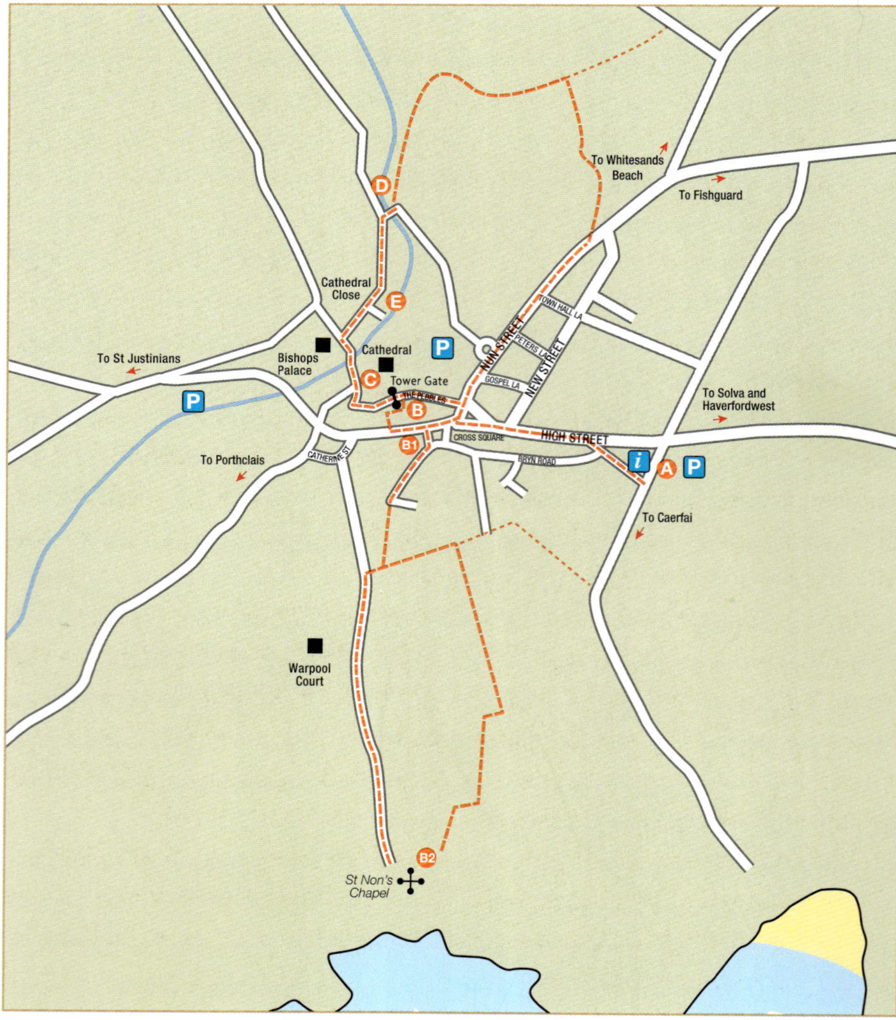
To Whitesands Beach
To Fishguard
D
Cathedral Close
E
To St Justinians
Bishops Palace
Cathedral
P
C
Tower Gate
THE PEBBLES
B
NUN STREET
TOWN HALL LA
PETERS LA
GOSPEL LA
NEW STREET
To Solva and Haverfordwest
P
B1
CROSS SQUARE
HIGH STREET
BRYN ROAD
CATHERINE ST
To Porthclais
i
A
P
To Caerfai
Warpool Court
B2
St Non's Chapel

Route

A) From the car park, walk, via the visitor centre towards the city centre, through the walled enclosure.

The walled enclosure behind the visitor centre was originally a tree-lined garden for the Grove Hotel opposite. The whitewashed roundabout, the Cocyn Round, was originally a mound of stones around which stagecoaches used to turn into the hotel for stabling. The hotel, in its time, has also been a private residence and housed a school.

Walking towards the Cross Square, the High Street is a mixture of traditional Welsh houses, some retaining their outer yards, and more modern building, although the pigsties of the nineteenth century have long since disappeared.

Many substantial Georgian buildings surround the Cross Square; Menevia House, to the left of the Cross Hotel, with its attractive shop window, was formerly a chemists, as was Court House on the left. Check the barometer there for impending weather; it was presented to the inhabitants of St Davids by the RNLI in 1872.

The lower part of what is now The Bishops Restaurant was built in 1778 and retains some of its grouted roof, as does the Oriel Gallery to the right. A distinctive feature of many traditional Pembrokeshire houses are their grouted roofs. The local slates, which were both heavy and relatively porous, were held down by rope or barbed wire and grouted with lime mortar over which successive layers of limewash were applied.

The Cross Hotel, the largest building on the square, and a former private residence, was originally ivy-clad and thatched, and dates from 1766. Many houses in St Davids also had their own wells, often located in cellars; some still retain them.

Optional route to St Nons from the Cross Square:

To visit St Nons Bay, which is a forty minute peaceful walk there and back, take the first exit off the Cross Square, signposted Porthclais and St

Justinians. Take the second road on the left, up Mitre Lane (B1). Turn right at the top, then after four hundred yards follow the grass path immediately left of the sign for Ffordd Owen. Turn right at the end of the track and left onto the road.

Return by the same route, turn left at the bottom of Mitre Lane, and then turn right along Tower Lane just past the Farmer's Arms to the Tower Gate (B).

For an alternative, rural route back from St Nons if the ground is fairly dry, turn left up the signposted footpath just after the St Nons Retreat Centre (B2), then left at the T-junction onto another path, and right along the fourth turning on the right, just before the road, joining the path on the outward route. Follow the directions as above to the Tower Gate. **Details of St Nons begin on page 29.**

St Davids Walk: *St Davids Cathedral*

B) From the Cross Square take the second exit down The Pebbles and through the Tower Gate. Follow the steps down to the cathedral.

As you pass under the fourteenth-century arch of the gateway of Porth y Twr, you enter nothing less than an ancient place of sanctity.

Porth y Twr, the Tower Gate, is one of four that stood as entrances to the cathedral close. The tower on the right houses the cathedral bells, and was built in the thirteenth century before the Close wall was created, at a greater height than the cathedral itself, for the bells to be heard more clearly.

The gateway originally had a portcullis and a gate, the ridges in the roof accommodating them can be seen, and a dungeon in the cellar under what is now the lapidarium to the left, described in 1811 by the historian Richard Fenton as, 'a dark, subterraneous vault or cavern with no other adit than a circular opening in the floor, covered with a strong grating of iron by which the malefactors were let into it.'

Today the gateway houses a collection some fine cross and circle incised stones dating from the ninth century, including early Christian ring cross stones from Pen Arthur farm, near Whitesands Bay. There is also an introductory exhibition to the cathedral and Close at the gateway. The lapidarium and exhibition are open in the holiday season.

The Close wall was created in the fourteenth century to separate the cathedral precinct from the secular world outside. It was also partly defensive in intent; some battlemented walls are still visible in the valley to the west. The buildings within the Close were created to house the clergy who served the cathedral.

The thirty-nine steps leading down to the cathedral are so named after the 'Thirty-Nine Articles of Religion' which were drawn up in 1563, outlining the basic summary of belief of the Church of England. The Church in Wales came into being in 1920.

When the kissing gate was replaced by a new gate in the early twentieth century the top step had to be taken away, and a new step was added at the bottom to keep the number of steps intact.[3]

The fields in the valley are those that David and his monks ploughed with yokes strapped to their backs in the sixth century, and jackdaws still clatter and crowd above a land of ancient spiritual veneration. Tradition has it that they never fly away from anyone dressed in black.

The cathedral stands on the site of David's original monastery, known in Irish in the late sixth century, as Cille Muine, the Cell of the Bush,[4] echoing the monastery's close links with Ireland and conveying a sense of the peace and natural abundance of the valley at the time that David created his monastic community here.

The name later evolved, in Welsh, to Mynyw, meaning a bush or grove, and in medieval times this became Latinised to Menevia. The present Welsh name for St Davids is Tyddewi, the House of David.

The site David chose in the beautiful valley was also on a pivotal point of communication and monastic travel on the western seaways.

The Abraham Stone

The site is midway between Porthclais Harbour for travel from the south and Whitesands Bay from the west and north. Many monks from Ireland, the West Country and Brittany would have visited.

After David's time the monastery at St Davids was frequently devastated and was attacked thirteen times between 878 and 1091, mainly by Vikings. Bishop Morgenau was killed in 999, which was looked upon as a punishment as he was the first bishop of St Davids to eat meat. On his last night he appeared in a vision to a certain bishop in Ireland, showing his wounds and saying, 'Because I ate flesh, I am become flesh.'

In 1080 Bishop Abraham's two sons were slaughtered; an intricately decorated, eleventh-century stone, now in the exhibition centre at the Tower Gate, commemorates these deaths.

In the medieval Life of St Caradog it is said that at some time towards the end of the eleventh century, owing to attacks of 'Viking pirates from the Orkneys', St Davids was left, 'without an inhabitant for seven years, so that a certain priest, after clearing away thorns and briars, hardly reached the tomb of the confessor on the seventh day.'

The Vikings had established Dublin as a major trading port, along with the east coast Irish ports of Waterford and Wexford. They also established significant bases in the Orkney Islands and the Isle of Man.

In 1081 William the Conqueror, a Viking descendant himself, made a more peaceful visit to St Davids. Already the Overlord of Wales and the most powerful man in the land, he paid homage at the sanctuary of David, accompanied by only a handful of foot-soldiers.

The visit made by this conqueror to David's shrine was recognition of his influence in the land, long after his death. Christians themselves, the Normans also saw the church as powerful and useful to them, but William

Spiritual Conflict

The astonishing era of the 'Age of the Saints', that from the fifth century saw the foundation of Celtic Christianity across the western seaboard, and was to flourish for two centuries, was not without its conflicts. When the adult David returned to his place of birth to found his monastic settlement it was not a move welcomed by all.

The sight of the smoke of a settlement from the valley so disturbed and incensed the family of his near neighbour, a chieftain named Boia, who is described as a druid and lived in a fort on a rocky outcrop at nearby Clegyr Boia, that his wife sent their daughters into the valley naked to divert David and his followers by, 'displaying love's seductive embraces', and indulging in, 'lewd talk.'

The monks were not to be diverted from their spiritual path, and Boia's wife then went to the valley with her stepdaughter, Dunod, and sat beneath a hazel tree, bidding her to lay her head on her lap under the guise of braiding her hair. She then cut off her head, and where her blood fell on the earth a spring was created. Known as Merthyr Dunod in medieval times, the spring was said, 'in abundance to cure many human sicknesses.' Its whereabouts today is unknown.

A short while later Boia perished in the Clegyr Boia fort in a fire, and his wife, it is said, went mad and fled, no-one knows where.

The tale is full of themes in Celtic folklore – the woodland with sacred hazel trees, the ceremonial dressing of hair, the miraculous spring, the smoke of settlement reminiscent of the more recent Welsh custom of 'Ty un nos', the right of claim to land and property through the lighting of a fire after creating a homestead in one night, and the sacrifice through beheading, a ritual said to have been undertaken in times of severe trouble and danger.

certainly had more motives for his visit.

This would have been a way of observing what was happening in an outlying part of the realm and of asserting power, including lordship, over the local chieftains.

He may also have seen the proximity of these shores as strategic to a future attack on Ireland and the Viking settlements on the east coast.

St Davids Cathedral has perhaps the most remote and elemental setting in Britain, not least with its backdrop of ancient hills. The mauve-tinged stone with which many of the walls are built, most vivid after rain, was quarried mainly from nearby Caerbwdy Bay.

The stone cathedral the Normans created is on the site of David's original wattle and daub monastic settlement; it is on boggy, sloping land, full of spring-water, hardly an enticing prospect for such great architects and their builders.

Entering the nave it is worth noting the slope of the floor, ascending by many feet from the west end to the high altar. This was extraordinarily difficult land on which to build.

Why did the Normans build it on this specific site, almost concealed from sight and also in such remote land? This cathedral is perhaps less an ostentatious display of power than a homage to a site regarded as a place of sanctity.

In 1131 the first stone cathedral was built in place of the wooden church.

The nave

Cathedral Guide

1 Font
2 Nave Altar
3 Rood Screen
4 St Caradog's Shrine
5 Chapel of St Thomas â Becket
6 Bishops Throne
7 St Davids Shrine
8 High Altar
9 Library
10 Chapel of the Holy Trinity
11 Chapel of St Nicholas
12 Chapel of St Edward

The twelfth-century nave is the most ancient area of the cathedral and dates from the rebuilding of the cathedral between 1181 and 1182.

The beautiful wooden ceiling is of Irish oak and was created in the sixteenth century, suspended by tie-beams to an upper ceiling. There is a local saying that no spider will spin a web on a nave ceiling of Irish oak.

The supporting columns of the nave lean outward, said to be due to inadequate foundations, the sloping and marshy ground, the weight of the tower and further movement caused by an earthquake in 1248. They do, however, lean with a harmonious symmetry that could denote a deliberate architectural design possibly with a weight bearing purpose. Norman chevrons, zig-zags and lozenges decorate the upper columns and arches.

The elaborate stone rood-screen was created by Bishop Gower in the fourteenth century, a visionary of architecture who was the major builder of the Bishop's Palace, contributing greatly to its spaciousness and elegance. His tomb is on the south side of the screen.

Walking left along the nave and past the rood-screen, the medieval shrine of St Caradog is on the right. St Caradog (died 1124) is one of the few Welsh saints to have lived after the Age of the Saints (400 to 600 AD), and spent much of his later life as a hermit by the Merlin's Brook just outside Haverfordwest before fulfilling his desire to be buried in the cathedral.

The tower lantern ceiling

The Chapel of St Thomas Becket has its origins in the early thirteenth century. Turning right just beyond the north transept and into the choir, it is well worth looking at the carved medieval misericords of the stalls. They were introduced by the early sixteenth century to relieve the clergy of standing for long periods of time; they would have appeared to be standing while in reality sitting.

The wooden carvings include two 'Green Men', thought to symbolise the coming of spring and hope and suggesting a medieval affinity with nature. There is also humour and a sense of shared humanity in depictions of seasickness and backache.

The choir includes a royal stall, reserved for the sovereign and occupied by Queen Elizabeth II in 1995, and the Bishop of St Davids' fourteenth-century, intricately carved wooden throne. Above is the beautiful tower lantern ceiling of intricate colour and design. Medieval in origin it was restored, with further decoration, in the nineteenth century.

Beyond the choir is St David's shrine, created in 1275, and recently restored in 2012. The shrine, and the relics themselves, have had a slightly mysterious history.

In 1087 David's shrine had been taken from the cathedral and stripped of its precious metals, possibly including bronze and silver; although the thieves are said to have emptied the shrine of its relics, their whereabouts remaining unknown for a time.

The present shrine was built following what was believed by some to be a re-discovery of St David's relics as a result of a vision by a prior in the thirteenth century that his body was buried outside the south porch.

An earlier shrine is thought to have been behind the high altar, accessed via a recess in what was originally an outer wall of the cathedral, now forming part of the sixteenth-century Holy Trinity Chapel.

During the Reformation, in 1536, Bishop Barlow removed the relics, thought to be of St David and his friend and confessor St Justinian, their fate remaining unknown but possibly destroyed as so many were at this time.

Then during restoration of the cathedral in 1866, the recess in the Holy Trinity Chapel, which had been blocked in the 1520s, was uncovered and bones were found, embedded in mortar for their preservation, on the sill. They were re-interred under the floor in the chapel and then recovered in 1920 to be placed inside two reliquaries in an oak chest in the recess.

The relics were radiocarbon-dated in 1997, revealing that they mainly date from the eleventh to the twelfth centuries, suggesting that they may well contain the bones of St Caradog who died in 1124. No relics were found to be from the sixth century, the time of St David and St Justinian. The reliquaries in the chest were moved to the present, restored shrine, in 2012, and the chest removed from the chapel.

Throughout the twelfth to the fifteenth centuries, thousands of pilgrims, particularly from across Britain and Ireland, were drawn to St David's shrine.

In recognition of the status and influence of the shrine at St Davids, Bishop Bernard of St Davids secured a canonization of David from Pope Calixtus II in 1123. The pontiff also decreed that two pilgrimages to St Davids were equal to one to Rome, ensuring the importance and significance of the shrine as a major centre of pilgrimage.

The practice of going on a pilgrimage is common to many religions, but it found a particular momentum in Europe at this time. The belief that pilgrimages to the place where a saint had lived, and in particular, to the shrine of a saint, could provide salvation in this life and the afterlife, was one that grew in impetus.

The relics of saints were revered as sources of healing, protection and redemption. It was believed that the power of a saint's holy life lay in his relics, and that prayers offered before a shrine might be granted. The belief in cures and miracles was widely held.

Pilgrims also went for a variety of individual and more secular reasons; noblemen to pray for victory in battle, farmers for the fertility of their land, women for children and ease in childbirth. The belief in pilgrimage ran throughout society and pilgrims were drawn from all walks of life, both rich and poor, royalty and peasantry.[5]

Monarchs made their way to St Davids in medieval times. King Henry II visited in 1171 and 1172; King John, King Edward I, King Richard II and his wife Queen Eleanor were also to pay homage at the saint's shrine.

One tradition has it that the entrance to the shrine for pilgrims was through the arched doorway in the west wall of the north transept, now the entrance to the Treasury. Writing in 1923 in the Twr-y-Felin Guide to St Davids, Henry Evans stated that 'until recently' there were tiles, hollowed by pilgrims on their knees, in the floor to the back of the shrine. The tiles, he added, had not long since been replaced.

Times were to change radically in the sixteenth century. 'No cathedral is more corrupt nor none so far out of its frame than St Davids,' Bishop William Barlow was to write after his election in 1536, 'it is an antique gargle of idolatry.'

Barlow was an enthusiastic Protestant, an active participant in the hammer blows of the Reformation after Henry VIII had broken from Rome in 1534. Pilgrimage was denounced as superstition and the great journeys to the shrine of Wales' patron saint were halted.

In his reforming zeal Barlow certainly had a way with words; he dismissed the relics in the cathedral as, 'two heads of silver plate enclosing two rotten skulls stuffed with petrified clouts; item, two arm bones, and a worm-eaten book covered with silver plate.' As well as removing the relics he stripped the jewels from the shrine. Could this specific reference to two skulls be an indication that they may have been those of St David and St Justinian?

More severe damage to the cathedral was to follow in the Civil War, in which north Pembrokeshire mainly took the Royalist side. It is said that in 1648 Oliver Cromwell rode his horse into the cathedral, and that the marks of the hooves are still there on some of the cracked fifteenth-century tiles of the presbytery before the high altar.

During the same year his parliamentary soldiers moved in. As well as using the cathedral for stabling, they stripped lead from the roof and other buildings in the Close, destroyed the stained glass windows and the organ, and ruined any vestiges of the medieval library left after the Reformation.

Not everyone was intimidated by this show of power and destruction. There is a tale of a young organist, who, overhearing Cromwell's soldiers in the choir discussing the destruction of the cathedral organ, threw a large stone at them from the upper gallery. When he was pursued he hid in a bell in the tower, hanging onto the clapper, and escaped detection.

The tomb in the centre of the presbytery is of Edmund Tudor, Henry VII's father. His remains and the tomb were placed here under the instructions of his grandson, Henry VIII. Edmund Tudor was partly of Welsh ancestry and his remains were moved here from Grey Friars Church in Carmarthen at the time of the Dissolution of the Monasteries.

The decision to move his grandfather's tomb here was, perhaps, a reflection of Henry VIII's own spiritual and political uncertainties at a time of great change that he did so much to instigate. Grey Friars Church was to suffer the same fate as the monasteries at the time his grandfather's tomb was moved.

Beyond the high altar the Holy Trinity Chapel, created in the sixteenth century over what was then an open courtyard, is a haven of peace. The recess, built into what was previously an outer wall, was very possibly the access point for pilgrims visiting St David's earlier shrine behind the high altar.

The south choir aisle

There is fine Perpendicular fan vaulting in the ceiling, and the altar contains a lovely amalgamation of medieval carved stones which were used in its reconstruction in the 1920s. Placed there at the same time were the twentieth century statues of Bishop Edward Vaughan, who constructed the chapel, and of Giraldus Cambrensis.

Giraldus Cambrensis, a fine historian in Wales of the twelfth century, sought in vain for an official canonization of St Caradog from Pope Innocent III, and for his own appointment as Bishop of St Davids. Despite offers

St Davids Walk: *St Nons Bay*

St Nons Well

St Nons Bay, in its own quiet, peaceful way, is a remarkable place. Ancient tradition has it that the birthplace of St David was where a ruined chapel now stands, looking across to the Atlantic. He was born during a thunderstorm, but at the moment of birth a shaft of serene light fell on mother and child.

The chapel is surrounded by scattered standing stones, the remains of a Bronze Age circle created 4,000 years ago. This is a site, blessed with a spring, that may well have been venerated for thousands of years.

Writing in 1954 in The Holy Wells of Wales, Francis Jones said that he had found nearly two hundred examples of chapels or churches built at or near wells in Wales, with thirty-three in Pembrokeshire.

The well is said to have been created at the moment of St David's birth, and traditionally heals rheumatism and diseases of the eye. In medieval times spring-water was taken from here to the cathedral and used as holy water to wash and purify St David's shrine.

It was believed by many pilgrims that the land in which a saint had lived was sanctified by his presence, and this was a place of pilgrimage second only to the cathedral.

The offerings were substantial. We are told that what was offered here and other chapels on the peninsula was carried, 'by dishfuls' to the cathedral and, 'divided every Saturday among the canons and priests . . . the quantity not allowing them leisure to tell it.'[8]

Just over the hedge in the chapel field are the remains of a rectangular building, possibly the well-keeper's cottage.

The well would almost certainly have had a more substantial enclosure around it than exists today. The present cowl over the well, medieval in design, dates from the eighteenth century and was restored in the last century.

According to local folklore, in the middle ages there were lime-washed standing stones marking the way from the cathedral close to the well. Could this indicate visits to the well at auspicious times, at night or dawn?

According to Francis Jones, in records from medieval times onwards, the most popular times for visits to wells in Wales were, 'night and morning, midnight, before sunrise, dawn, and while the dew was still on the ground.'

In Pembrokeshire it was believed that young women would retain the beauty of their complexions by bathing their faces in dew before sunrise on May Day, the beginning of the Celtic summer festival of Beltane.[9]

It is thought that Bronze Age circles, often aligned with the movements of the sun and moon, particularly at times of solstice and equinox, and possibly with the passage of stars, were used to calculate the timing of auspicious times of the year, both as a homage to the seasonal passage of the earth, and more practically, for predicting the changing seasons and the processes of the farming cycle.

They would have also have been places of ritual, possibly including worship of fertility, birth and growth. Is it a coincidence that the reputed birthplace of St David lies within the remains of a Bronze Age circle?

Even after the Reformation local people continued to give offerings and make their prayers here, and elsewhere in Wales; the people were slow to follow the Protestantism of their leaders. A letter written at the end of the sixteenth century said of the Welsh:

'They doe still goe in heapes one pilgrimage to the wonted welles and places of superstition; and in the nightes after the feastes when the ould offringes were used to be kept at anie chappell, albeit the church be pulled down, yet doe they come to the place where the church or chappell was, by great journeys barefoots.'[10]

Browne-Willis wrote of St Nons in 1715, 'There is a fine well . . . cover'd with a Stone-Roof, and inclosed within a wall, with Benches to sit upon round the Well. Some old simple People go still to visit this Saint at some particular Times, especially upon St Nun's Day (March 2nd) which they keep holy, and offer Pins, Pebbles, Etc at this well.'

In 1811 Richard Fenton wrote, 'The fame this consecrated spring had obtained is incredible, and is still resorted to for many complaints. In my infancy, as was the general usage with respect to children at that time, I was often dipped in it, and offerings, however trifling, even of a farthing or a pin, were made after each ablution, and the bottom of the well shone with votive brass.'

St Nons Chapel

The chapel in the field is unusual as it is orientated north-south rather than east-west in the traditional Christian church and chapel settings towards the dawning and setting sun. Like the cathedral it is built on sloping ground; it would have been much more practical to build it further up the field where the ground is more level. Is it possible that the building, whatever its earliest origins, was situated to be within the Bronze Age circle?

Standing stone in St Nons Chapel

The circle and cross incised standing stone in the corner of the chapel possibly dates from the seventh or eighth century, and is beautiful in its harmony and symmetry, incorporating the two most universal symbols, the circle and the quadrant, and possibly symbolic of the passage from a pagan belief to a Christian one.

It is not known where it is from, or how it came to be placed here but it is possible that it was originally a stone in the Bronze Age circle.

Look south-west across the Atlantic from the chapel and the nearest landfall is Latin America. The curve of St Brides Bay is visible from here, named after the sixth-century Irish saint, Brigid, in whose famous monastery in Kildare a perpetual fire was kept lit. Ireland lies to the north-west.

The Catholic chapel outside the Retreat Centre was built in 1934, emulating medieval chapels in the area and using many stones from the former Whitewell Priory which was located near the road leading up to St Nons, and of which there is no trace.

The altar incorporates much medieval stonework and a white quartz stone from St Patricks Chapel at Whitesands Bay, one of many discovered during an excavation in 1924. The holy water stoup is said to be from Capel y Gwrhyd, a medieval chapel near Rhodiad y Brenin just outside St Davids, and of which virtually only the site now remains.

St David

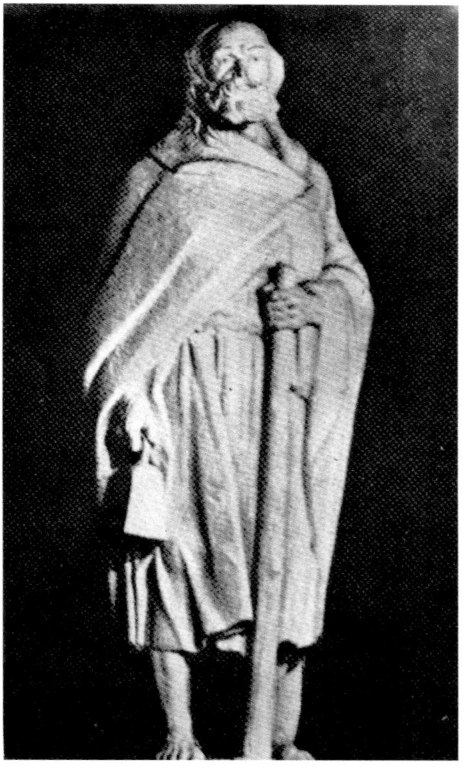

Sculpture of St David at Llandewi Brefi Church, Ceredigion

A tall, barefoot priest who wore rough, animal clothing, lived on bread, water and herbs, and created a monastic community of intense spirituality and devotion to God, the influence of St David on the spiritual and cultural unity of Wales has been profound.

The seat of worship that he established led to the present cathedral that bears his name, perhaps the most beautiful in Wales.

What we know of this patron saint comes largely from the writings of his life, written around 1090 by the scholarly Rhygyfarch, son of the St David's Bishop, Sulien.

In The Life of David, Rhygyfarch says that he drew on 'very old writings' that were in existence particularly at the monastery of St Davids, including some in David's own hand, and written, 'in the old style of the ancients'.

Written some five centuries after David's life, this account was no doubt motivated in favour of the Welsh church against the changes to be wrought by the Christian Norman invader, but scholars agree that elements of the Life contain much more than a grain of truth.

Of an aristocratic heritage, David's mother, Non, is said to have conceived after being raped by Sant, the king of the ancient tribal kingdom of Ceredigion.

His date of birth is thought to be around 500 AD and he is reputed to have been born at St Nons during a thunderstorm, and yet, 'the place wherein the mother cried in her travail shone with so serene a light that it glistened as though the sun was visible and God had brought it in front of the clouds.' At that moment a pure spring rose from the ground nearby.

St Nons Bay

David was well-educated, and became renowned as a preacher and teacher, founding churches and monastic settlements throughout south Wales and in south-west England. There are over fifty church dedications to St David in south Wales.

With many Irish settlers in south west Wales from the fourth century onwards, it is possible that he spoke Irish as well as Latin and an early form of Welsh. Close links with Ireland are also revealed in the Lives of Irish saints, in which many visits to St Davids are recounted.

After much travel, it is claimed that, with his contemporaries, Teilo and Padarn, he even visited Jerusalem. David was directed by an angel to create the monastery in Glyn Rhosyn, the Valley of the Little Marsh, where the cathedral now stands.

Christianity in this era on the western seaboard of Europe was a mix of missionary travel, monasticism and solitude, inspired, in particular, by early Christians of the Near East who moved to the deserts of Egypt and Syria from the third to the sixth century.

Known as the Desert Fathers, they had initially fled from persecution in the Roman provinces of Egypt and the Near East. When Christianity became the official religion of Imperial Rome in the fourth century, this was perceived as a barrier to the authentic practice of their faith.

They looked for something closer to the source of their faith, for meditation, peace and solace in the desert. Many were to come together in groups for worship, creating the first Christian monastic settlements.

From here the influence of monasticism spread westwards and was practised, particularly widely, in Gaul.

Many here also sought spiritual solace in nature and remote places. Rhygyfarch says of David at his monastery that, 'in imitating the Egyptian monks he led a similar life to theirs.'

Rhygyfarch gives us a vivid account of this sixth-century Christian monastery, one devoted to prayer, humility, labour and the needs of others.

Ploughing without oxen, he says that the monks, 'place the yoke on their shoulders; with unwearied arm they dig into the ground with mattocks and spades . . . they provide with their own labour all the necessities of the community.'

When the work was done, 'no complaint was heard, no conversation was held beyond what was necessary. But each did the task enjoined either with prayer or well-directed meditation.'

When the labour was finished, the rest of the day was spent in reading, writing or prayer. At the approach of evening a bell was rung and the monks proceeded to the church where they worshipped, 'on bended knees until the stars are seen in heaven bringing the day to a close.'

After supper was taken they returned to the church for three hours, 'insistent' in watchings, prayers and genuflexions.

Possessions were regarded with disdain, 'they reject the gifts of the unjust; they detest riches.' Everything in the community was for the common good, nothing was 'mine' or 'thine'.

We can speculate from this that David would not have viewed a person's contribution and entry to the monastery in terms of money, gifts of objects or land, but wholly in terms of their spiritual commitment. We are also told that those who wished to join the monastery had to remain outside for ten days before being accepted into the community.

An important function, led by David, was to feed a multitude of the bereft, orphans, widows, the needy, the weak, the infirm and pilgrims who gathered daily outside the monastery walls.

There would have been many visitors from across the western seaboard in this Age of the Saints. Rhygyfarch relates that, 'the report of Holy David's name was heard abroad, the kings and princes of this world were encouraged to abandon their kingdoms for the monastic life as did Constantine, king of the Cornishmen.'

David came to be known as 'The Waterman', partly from his insistence on drinking only water, but also, after early service and then, 'proceeding alone to angelic discourse', from his ritual of standing in cold water for long periods of time.

In some cultures immersion in water is seen as a way of cooling the liver, which is regarded as a significant process in spiritual development. He may well have immersed himself in the sea, and bathing in salt water is also widely regarded as a form of purification.

David could be described as the tribal head of his church and monastery, close to nature and the land where he settled, bareheaded, barefooted, carrying a staff of wood fashioned from a branch, and a bell, 'Bangu', the 'dear loud one', which is said to have possessed magical powers.

According to Rhygyfarch he is said to have triumphed over the 'heresy' of Pelagianism at a large gathering at Llandewi Brefi in mid Wales, where he was invited to preach. Pelagianism denied the doctrine of original sin, stating that people have free will and can achieve salvation through their own efforts.

However, the historian Nora Chadwick has pointed out that the only authority for such an important meeting comes from Rhygyfarch himself, who was seeking to enhance David's authority among his people in the face of the Norman advance.

It is also curious that David would preach, effectively in support of Rome, against such a movement that itself had Celtic roots. Pelagius was a Celt, thought to be Welsh or possibly Scottish, who became involved in the controversy while staying in Rome at around 415 AD.

It is related that David came reluctantly, but that a mound grew under his feet as he preached, enabling him to be seen and heard by the crowds that had gathered there. Llandewi Brefi church stands on the site.

After a second important meeting at Llandewi Brefi, seeking to restore order after a great pestilence in 547 AD, David was proclaimed, in Rhygyfarch's medieval terms, 'archbishop' of Wales, 'the chief overseer of all, the chief protector, the chief spokesman, from whom all received the rule and model of right living.' And that, 'Everywhere sounds of prayers are raised to the stars . . . with what blaze of miracles he shone!'

It is said that David lived for over one hundred years, and that he died on the 1st March, now St David's Day, in 589 or 602 AD.

Some of his last words are said to have been, 'Be joyful, and keep your faith and your creed. Do the little things that you have seen me do and heard about. I will walk the path that our fathers have trod before us.' At his burial the monastery was filled with angels as Christ received his soul.

Porthclais Harbour

Caerfai, St Nons and Porthclais

A walk along coastline and inland rural paths with spectacular views of the sweep of St Brides Bay and the islands beyond, passing the peaceful beauty of St Nons Bay and the ancient harbour of St Davids at Porthclais. The return is along an inland rural path.

Time: Two hours

Distance: Two and a half miles

Terrain: Moderate walking with an initial, short road section, and along coastline and rural paths. One short, steepish incline. The route back in very wet weather is muddy in parts, but passable with appropriate footwear. Also in wet weather in the early summer when the foliage is at its highest, waterproof trousers are recommended for this section of the walk.

Take care with young children on the road to Caerfai, which is busy in the summer, and areas of the coast where the path gets close to the cliff edge, between St Nons Bay and Porthclais.

Facilities: Cafes, pubs, restaurants in St Davids, refreshment kiosk at Porthclais in the summer. WC in St Davids and Porthclais.

Getting there: On the Haverfordwest road at the top of the High Street, take the signposted road for Caerfai SA62 6QT. Parking at the visitor centre car park SA62 6NW, or at Caerfai with limited spaces in the summer.

Public transport: None to Caerfai. The Celtic Coaster, pick up point at Porthclais.

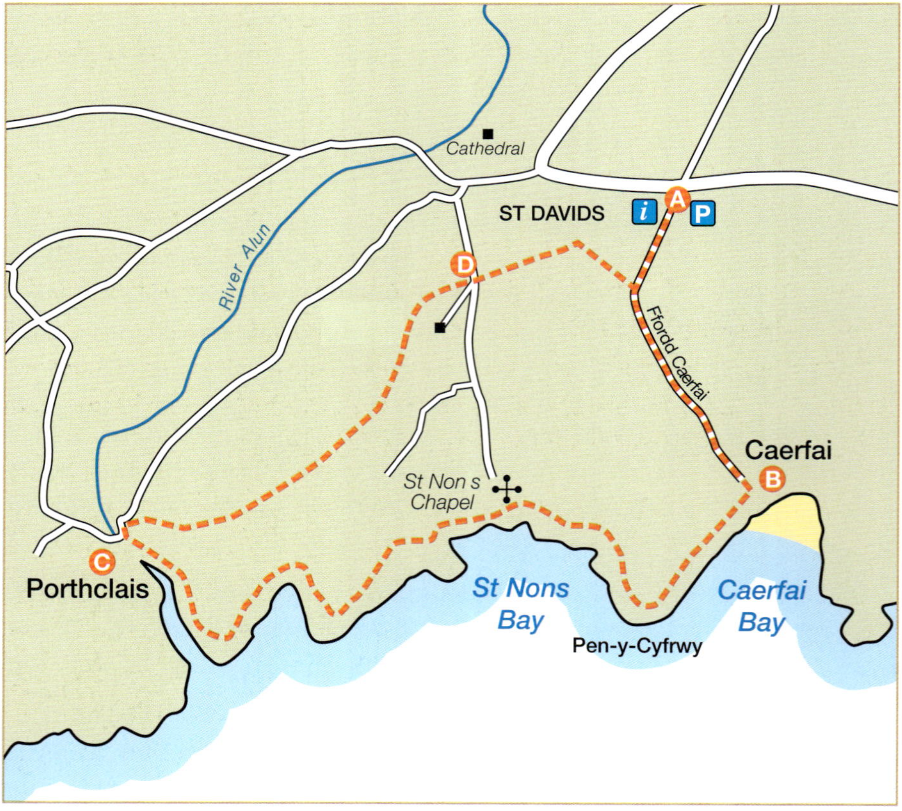
Cathedral
ST DAVIDS
A
P
i
River Alun
D
Ffordd Caerfai
Caerfai
B
St Non s
Chapel
C
Porthclais
St Nons
Bay
Caerfai
Bay
Pen-y-Cyfrwy

Route

A) From the visitor centre car park turn left and follow the minor road to Caerfai Bay. The large building on the left was originally built as a windmill in 1806, one of two in the area. It became a hotel in 1904.

B) At Caerfai Bay car park, turn right onto the coast path, heading north. As you approach St Nons Bay take care as the path gets close to the cliff edge.

Caerfai has fine, firm sand below high tide. Much of the mauve-tinged stone for the cathedral has been quarried from here and Caerbwdi Bay, to the south, over the centuries. Driftwood from Latin America has been found on the beach here. A little way along the path there are wonderful views of the sweep of St Brides Bay and Skomer Island.

As you pass the small headland of Pen-y-Cyfrwy, the islands south of Ramsey Island are visible in the distance. The twin hills of the island seem still part of a mainland to which they once belonged.

Islands at the south end of Ramsey Island

Details of St Nons are on page 29. It is well worth diverting inland after the retreat centre here to visit St Nons Well and the ruined chapel of St David's reputed birthplace. Take the path straight on below the retreat centre that runs past the chapel.

Porthclais Harbour

The whitewashed cottage visible as you round the headland of Porth Clais is a traditional Pembrokeshire cottage with its grouted roof, small windows and large porch.

An interpretation for the name, Porth Clais, is 'the harbour of the clas'.[10] 'Clas' is a term for the earliest monastic communities in west Wales. There would have been much passage through the harbour in the Age of the Saints, both to and from St David's monastery.

Porthclais must have been in use as a harbour and inlet since boats were created. Norman in origin, the harbour wall was extensively restored in 1722.

Records show boats arriving with cargoes for the repair and refurbishment of the cathedral in 1385, including fifteen poles for scaffolding from Ireland, and iron, lead, limestone and coal from the south of the county.[11]

In later centuries oats, barley, malt and wool were exported to Bristol, north Wales and Wexford in Ireland, returning with cargoes of hops, raisins, calico, pepper, salt and Irish timber. Irish oak for the ceiling in the cathedral nave may well have passed through Porthclais in the late sixteenth century.

By the seventeenth century corn was the major export. Barley, wheat and rye were regularly carried to Bristol, Barnstaple and north Wales; the ships returning with all kinds of general merchandise including timber, hops and cloth, a miscellany of household goods and wine from Bristol. Cargoes were unloaded at low tide onto waiting carts.

In the early nineteenth century trade was significant. In 1830 three thousand quarters of grain and two hundred and fifty casks of butter were shipped to the West Country.[12]

With the coming of the railways in the 1850s trade by sea was rapidly coming to an end, and with the arrival in the 1920s of transport by road, sea trade on the peninsula was over, ending an era, stretching thousands of years, of travel, trade and communication by sea.

A Tale of King Arthur

In the Mabinogion, the earliest book of Welsh tales, King Arthur is said to have landed at Porthclais from Ireland in pursuit of the monstrous boar, Twrch Trwyth, a former prince turned into a boar for his misdeeds.

Twrch Trwyth was accompanied by seven young pigs and carried a golden comb, shears and a razor between his ears.

In order to marry his love, Olwen, her father, the giant Ysbaddaden, had set Arthur's nephew, Culwch, a number of tasks including the retrieval of the golden objects from Twrch Trwyth to be used to cut and groom the boar's hair.

Arthur accompanied him, and after a skirmish in the nearby Preseli Hills, the giant boar was pursued to Cornwall. After all the objects were retrieved, Twrch Trwyth disappeared into the sea, and Culwch returned to Ireland to marry Olwen.

The hoop-shaped buildings at the head of the harbour are limekilns, in use from 1650 to 1906, all with ramps leading up one side to barrow up loads of anthracite and limestone to fill the kilns from the top. Beyond the second limekiln above the harbour wall there was a pub, of which no trace remains.

Lime for the Land

Lime was used to fertilize the acid soil of the land, or as a mortar and limewash for buildings. Crushed limestone, anthracite dust and shale waste was brought from quarries in the south of the county, and loaded in layers onto a base of tightly packed gorse. The heat resulted in quicklime which was pushed out of the kiln through the apertures at the base.

Beyond the kilns on the other side of the harbour are the remains of the limeburner's cottage, now nearly covered with undergrowth. It was built to be out of the path of the toxic fumes that the kilns produced.

Just beyond the upper car park are the remains of a well, Ffynnon Ddewi, David's Well. This was the site of St David's baptism by St Aelvyw, later to become Bishop of Munster, who had arrived from Ireland at the harbour.

The well-water is said to have miraculously sprung up for the baptism. It is particularly clear and pure, and there is a local saying for fine drinking water, 'As pure as Dewi's well'.

Beyond the well and hidden from site by undergrowth is the site of an ancient chapel, Capel y Pistyll, the Chapel of the Water Spout. In 1715 Browne Willis described the chapel as having the water from the spring running underneath it into, 'a cistern at ye east end under ye pinion or gable of ye building.' It is still remembered today that the water fell into a well-worn cupped stone. The brick walls beside the car park are the remains of the St Davids gasworks, which operated from 1900 to 1960.

C) Take the path to the right just beyond the gates to the harbour entrance and up the wooden-faced steps. Follow the yellow footpath signs inland and walk across the camp site towards the white farmhouse. Turn left before the farmhouse on the tarmac road for five yards, then turn right.

D) When you reach the tarmac road you can turn left down the road into St Davids or go straight across the road along the footpath which meets the Caerfai Bay road. Turn left here and back to the visitor centre car park.

The inland path back was formerly known as the Captain's Way, as it was the route sailors took to walk from St Davids to Porthclais. The fine building on the right was originally built in 1870 to accommodate and educate choristers of the St Davids Cathedral School.

St Davids to Solva

A highly recommended route is to turn left at Caerfai Bay and follow the coast path to Solva (four miles, three hours), with plenty of cafes and pubs, and return by the Richards Brothers bus service to St Davids or the Puffin Shuttle.

Places and sights to visit

Map page 48

All have ample parking except where otherwise indicated.
Postcodes are included where possible.

Carreg Samson burial chamber

Recommended visits

❶ St Nons – Reputed birthplace of St David, ancient well and chapel above the cliffs. Celtic Coaster. Walk page 29.

❷ Porthclais – Harbour for St Davids with an ancient history. WC. Refreshments in the summer. SA62 6RR. Celtic Coaster. Walk page 38.

❸ St Justinians – Lifeboat station, wonderful views across Ramsey Sound. SA62 6PY. Limited parking. Celtic Coaster. Walk page 54.

❹ Solva – Fjord-like harbour, now bustling with yachts. Pubs, cafes, restaurants. SA62 6UU. Puffin Shuttle and hourly bus service.

❺ Porthgain – Harbour with quarrying industrial history and workings in an evocative setting. Pub, restaurant. WC. SA62 5BL. Strumble Shuttle. Walk page 86.

❻ Abereiddy and the Blue Lagoon – A bay and beach with a former slate quarry with workings, buildings and housing. The Blue Lagoon is a former quarry formed into a deep lagoon by blasting the sea entrance, a short walk north from the beach. WC. SA62 6DT. Strumble Shuttle. Walk page 86.

❼ Abercastle – Lovely little harbour, once a place of prosperous sea trade. WC. Limited parking in the summer. SA62 5HJ. Strumble Shuttle. Walk page 88.

Ancient chapels and churches

❽ St Nons Chapel – Ancient ruined chapel and twentieth century chapel built in a medieval style above the cliffs. Celtic Coaster. Walk page 29.

The St Davids Peninsula

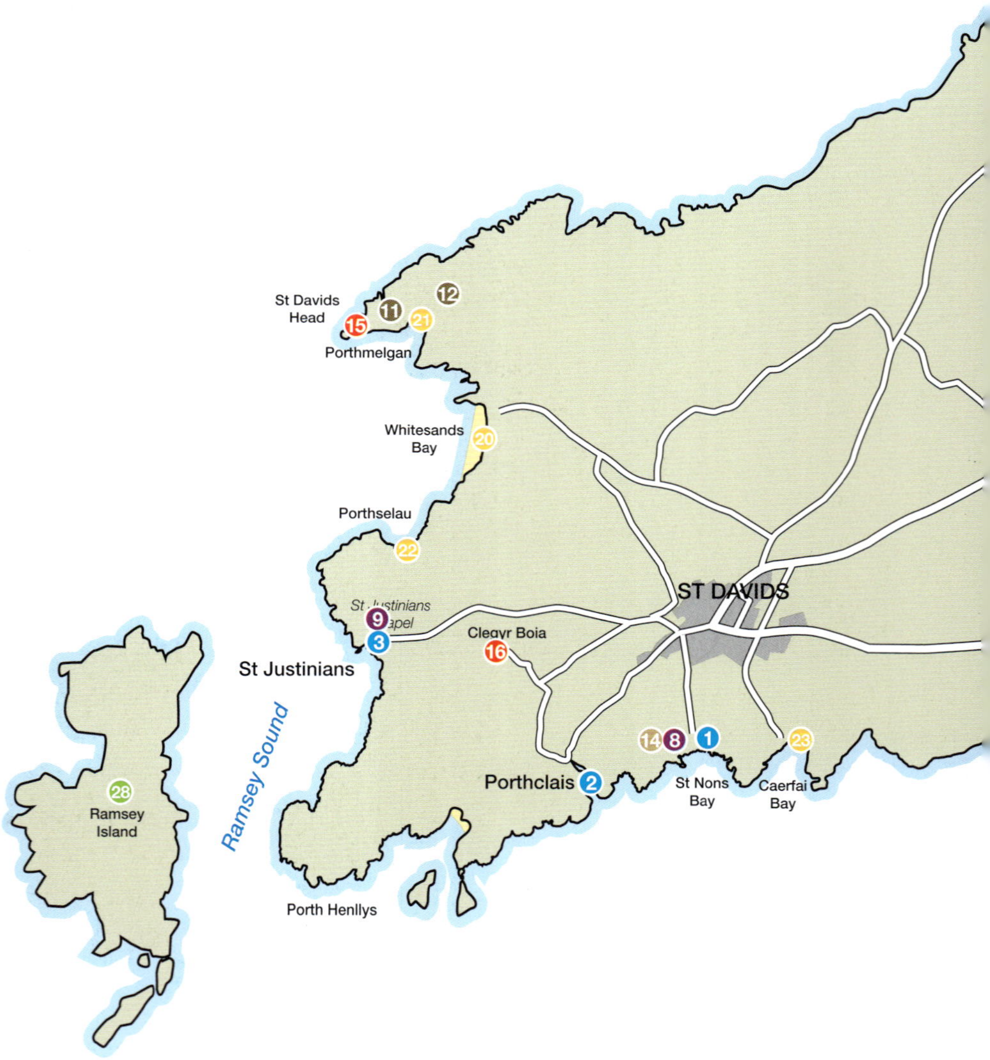

27
Abercastle
7
18
Trefin
13
5
Porthgain
26
6
25
Abereiddy
Llanrhian
Square and Compass
19
Croesgoch
Berea
Tretio
Carnhedryn
10
Caerfarchell
Middle Mill
Whitchurch
Wells
Upper Solva
Solva
4
17
St Elvis
Pointz Castle
Penycwm
Newgale
24

❾ St Justinians Chapel – No access but can be viewed from the roadside. Fine, but now roofless medieval chapel, dedicated to St Justinian, friend of St David. SA62 6PY. Limited parking. Celtic Coaster. Walk page 54.

❿ Llanhowel Church – Ancient site dedicated to sixth century St Hywel, contemporary of St David. Semi-circular graveyard. Possible former small monastery. Fine standing stone with Latin inscription thought to be sixth century. Signposted six miles from St Davids on the St Davids to Fishguard road.

Neolithic burial chambers

⓫ Coetan Arthur – Burial chamber on the approach to St Davids Head. Half an hour walk along the coast path from Whitesands Bay. Celtic Coaster. Walk page 64.

⓬ Carn Llidi – Two small burial chambers on the slopes of Carn Llidi. Walk page 64.

⓭ Carreg Samson – Fine burial chamber. Parking on the grass verge by the lane to Longhouse Farm, on the Trefin to Abercastle coast road. Footpath access along the lane. Can also be visited from Abercastle, SA62 5HJ, by coast path, limited parking. Parking also possible in Trefin, SA62 5AL, with a walk along a country road.

Note the careful positioning of two different types of stone in the chamber, the use of large stones in the wall opposite, taken from the chamber, and the angle of the capstone emulating the hill beyond, best viewed from the farm above. Strumble Shuttle to Trefin and Abercastle. Walk page 88.

Bronze Age standing stones

⑭ St Nons – The remains of a stone circle surrounding a ruined chapel above the cliffs. Celtic Coaster. Details page 29.

Iron Age forts

⑮ St Davids Head – Fine promontory fort in a wild, windswept location. Accessed by a half-hour walk along the coast path from Whitesands Bay, SA62 6PS, turn north at the beach. Celtic Coaster. Walk page 65.

⑯ Clegyr Boia – Originally a Neolithic settlement, then an Iron Age hill fort reputedly occupied by an Irish chieftain, Boia, who confronted St David, see page 17. The cathedral and its valley setting is clearly visible from here. No parking, it is best accessed by walking from St Justinians, SA62 6PY. Take the first turning right from St Justinians, lovely walk by Pwll Trefeiddan, an area of marshland. Can also be accessed from Porthclais, SA62 6RR. Celtic Coaster to St Justinians and Porthclais. Walk page 54.

⑰ Porth y Rhaw – Fine, multiple-banked promontory fort, forcing any approach into many S-turns. Take care at the cliff edge as it is eroding. Access on the coast path from St Davids or Solva.

⑱ Castell Coch – Evocative promontory fort with triple banks and ditches set above high, sheer cliffs. Nearest access from Abercastle, SA62 5HJ, very limited parking in the summer, or a longer route from Trefin, SA62 5AL. The coast path in this area is beautiful but narrow at times above steep cliffs, not suitable for children. Strumble Shuttle to Abercastle and Trefin. Walk page 88.

19 Caerau – Promontory fort with multiple banks and ditches. Access on the coast path west from Abereiddy, SA62 6DT, walk up the road and turn right. A lovely walk, but with steep cliffs, not suitable for young children. The little, pebbled cove of Caerau is fifteen minutes walk beyond the fort. Strumble Shuttle.

Beaches

20 Whitesands – A beautiful beach with fine sand, half a mile wide and backed by sand dunes. Lovely views of offshore islands. Rockpools at low tide, surfing, surf hire, cafe, wonderful coast walks. WC. West facing. Beach views from the car park. SA62 6PS. Celtic Coaster.

21 Porth Melgan – A lovely little cove a half-mile walk north from Whitesands. Fine sand below high tide. Watch for a sudden drop in depth if swimming. Facing south-west.

22 Porthselau – A sandy beach at all tides with good swimming and rock-pools. Two hundred yards wide. Facing north-west. Access is a short walk south from Whitesands.

23 Caerfai – The nearest beach to St Davids. South facing and protected by high cliffs, this two hundred yard wide, sandy beach, is often sheltered. Good swimming. Beach views from the car park, limited parking in the summer. SA62 6QT.

24 Newgale – A two mile stretch of white sand, Newgale is the biggest beach on the peninsula with a pebble-bank created by a great storm in 1859. Surfing and surf hire, cafes and a pub. WC. Facing south-west. Beach views from the middle car park. SA62 6AS. Puffin Shuttle and hourly bus service.

25 Abereiddy – Dark sanded, five hundred yards wide with lovely coastal walks. Difficult swimming, particularly in large sea swells, with many rocks. Evocative former slate quarrying works and buildings. WC. West facing. Beach views from the car park. Strumble Shuttle. Limited parking in the summer. SA62 6DT.

26 Traeth Llyfn – A beautiful beach, six hundred yards wide, with fine sand. Reached along a long flight of steps. Watch for currents and undertows if swimming in larger sea swells. Access only along the coast path from Abereiddy, SA62 6DT, or Porthgain, SA62 5BL. West facing. Strumble Shuttle to Abereiddy and Porthgain.

27 Abermawr – Backed by woods and a pebble-bank this north-west facing beach is protected from the prevailing south-westerly winds. Six hundred yards wide with fine sand from mid to low tide. Good swimming. Limited parking in the summer.

~~~~~~~~~

28 Ramsey Island – RSPB sanctuary a mile offshore, wild and beautiful, formerly farmed. A haven for Atlantic grey seals. Boats trips to and around the island, details at the St Davids Visitor Centre.
~~~~~~~~~

St Justinians

St Justinians and Porthclais

This, the longest of the circular routes, takes in the wild sweep of Ramsey Sound with spectacular views of the island, the remote beach of Porthlysgi and the beauty of Porthclais harbour.

You return inland along country roads, past the granite outcrop of Clegyr Boia, once a Neolithic and Iron Age settlement, a place of myth and legend with wonderful views of St Davids and across the peninsula, to the lifeboat station at St Justinians, perched above some of the most treacherous waters off the coast of Wales.

Time: Four hours.

Distance: Five and a half miles, with some shorter routes.

Terrain: Moderate walking along coastline and rural roads with some minor inclines, and one short hill on the road up from Porthclais. The path gets close to the cliff edge in parts of this walk.

Facilities: Refreshment kiosk in the summer at Porthclais. WC at Porthclais.

Getting there: From the Cross Square in St Davids take the first exit, signposted St Justinians SA62 6PY, turn right at the bottom of the hill, signposted St Justinians, and stay on the road for two miles. There is limited parking and the Celtic Coaster is recommended.

Public transport: The Celtic Coaster runs from St Davids to St Justinians. There are also pick-up points for returning to St Davids at Porthclais and at the Pencarnan sign on the road back to St Justinians.

St Justinians Chapel
Rhosson Farm
E
Clegyr Boia
P
A
St Justinians
D
Carn Trefeiddan
Ramsey Sound
Castell Heinif
C
Porthclais
Carn ar Wig
Treginnis Isaf
Melyn
B
Porthlysgi
Porth Henllys
Porthtaflod
Carreg Frân

Route

A) Turn left at the coast path above the St Justinians lifeboat station and follow the path for three and a half miles to the harbour of Porthclais.

The well on the left of the hill is named after St David's friend and confessor, St Justinian. He lived the latter part of his life as the head of a monastery on Ramsey Island, but, legend tells us, he considered that he had too many visitors and prayed that the rocky causeway across from the mainland would disappear.

A giant axe appeared for him to cut the causeway away, leaving only a jagged line of rocks towards the island as the axe became blunter. You can see these rocks, now known as The Bitches, where a fast flowing current suddenly gets faster, just below Ramsey's white farmhouse.

The ruined sixteenth-century chapel on the right was built under the guidance of Bishop Gower, who designed the Bishop's Palace. Dedicated to St Justinian, it is possibly on the site of an earlier chapel. It is said that St Justinian was buried here before his remains were moved to the cathedral; the outline of an early grave lies within the chapel.

St Justinians Chapel

Legend has it that St Justinian was beheaded on the island by the monks, who found the discipline of his monastery too strict, and that he walked miraculously back across the Sound to the mainland with his head under his arm. He laid it down at the site of the chapel before finally giving up his life.

St Justinians has housed lifeboats since 1869 and saved over three hundred lives. Imagine putting to sea under oar in the nineteenth century at night in a winter gale. The first lifeboat, the Augusta, required a crew of ten oarsmen, three officers, coxswain, second coxswain and bowman. From 1869 to 1885 she saved twenty-three lives.[13]

The new lifeboat station was built to accommodate the 25-knot Tamar class lifeboat, Norah Whitley, and became operational in October 2016.

St Justinians lifeboat stations, old and new

Turning south from the new lifeboat station, as you approach a natural arch of pink and red sandstone jutting into the sea, the main path passes along the deeply dug ditch between twin embankments of the Iron Age fort, Castell Heinif.

The clear, blue-green waters of the Sound lap the rocks of the mainland. Gorse flourishes on this stretch of coast, a beautiful riot of scented yellow above the tidal races.

As you approach the little cove of Carn ar Wig look down to the right and opposite the cove a small concrete quay and winch can be seen. These date from the 1920s to serve boats crossing to and from Ramsey Island. This deep anchorage is known to have been used from the thirteenth century.

Ramsey Island, now an RSPB nature reserve, was farmed until 1968 and from early medieval times was known to have been very productive.

In 1280 there were seventy goats and forty-four horned cattle on the island, with thirty acres devoted to the growing of oats, wheat and barley.[14] In recent centuries the major exports to the mainland were sheep, wool, butter, cheese and corn.

Ramsey had earlier inhabitants; there are Bronze Age burial cairns on the island's twin hills, and the remains of Iron Age or even earlier field enclosure walls, most clearly visible to the south-west of the island.

Tradition has it that there was once a very early Christian monastery on the island, founded by St Dyfanog. The earliest name for the island is Ynys Tyfanog, St Dyfanog's Island. Early Christian stone coffins have been found on the possible site, near to the present whitewashed farmhouse.

There was also a healing well, probably at the spring just north of the farmhouse, which became a focus of much medieval pilgrimage. The historian John of Tynemouth wrote in the fourteenth century that the water, 'quaffed by sick folk, conveys health of body to all.' It is said that a man suffering from a swelling in his stomach, drank from it, became very sick, then threw up a frog, and was cured immediately.[15]

Analysis of an airborne laser survey of the island in 2017 revealed more evidence of a Bronze Age community that lived there some 4,500 years ago. The survey discovered further Bronze Age burial cairns, a prehistoric coastal promontory fort, the possible site of a Christian chapel dedicated to St Dyfanog near to the farmhouse and evidence of extensive medieval farming practice.

The island is a favoured breeding ground for Atlantic grey seals and about two hundred pups are born there each year. Calving takes two weeks on land above the high tide line. The pupping season begins in August and ends by early November, and seals are often seen off the mainland.

The path curves right and left to Penmaen Melyn, the most westerly point on the peninsula, with wonderful views across the Sound to the line of The Bitches rocks. Even on the calmest days the torrent of water plunging through these treacherous rocks can be heard. Porpoises and dolphins often pass through the Sound.

At the bottom of a short incline opposite The Bitches are the remains of a copper mine, opened by two Scottish brothers of Treginnis Farm in 1829 and abandoned in 1836. One of the two shafts and the remains of a shed, a retaining wall and a level working platform, are visible.

After the path turns east above the small bay of Porthtaflod there was another shaft, just above the mound of stones. The shaft was opened in 1833 and closed in 1889 following a fatal accident when a workman fell to the bottom of the shaft. In all there were seven shafts sunk for copper and lead ore in this area of the coast.

There are wonderful views of the small islands at the south end of Ramsey, framing a view of Grassholm Island in the distance. Home to a huge gannet colony, Grassholm is the third largest colony in the world, with 39,000 nesting pairs.

Gannets are a familiar sight along the coast with their distinctive yellow casts over neck and head, long, sharp beaks and round-hooped, penetrating eyes. Capable of diving from up to one hundred feet with wings pinned back to catch its prey, a shadow of movement below the water's surface, the eyesight of a gannet is twelve times as powerful as our own.

B) For a short-cut, turn left above Porth Henllys up the wooden-faced steps and past the white cottage. Turn right over the stile, then left in front of the white farmhouse. Where the track veers left or right, go right and follow the path down to the coast. Along the coast path there is also a good rural path back the top of the hill above St Justinans, turn right at the second National Trust sign for Trefeiddan, beyond the Castell Heinif Iron Age fort.

There is also a route from Treginnis Isaf to Clegyr Boia (D). Turn right at the white farmhouse and walk along the farm track and the minor road turning left at the crossroads.

The earliest historical reference to the farm dates from 1283 in the list of the manors of St Davids. It is now a 'Farm for City Children', a charity set up to give children from urban areas experience of farming life.

Enchanted Island

As with many islands, Grassholm was a land of enchantment for the Celts. In the Mabinogion, Bran the Blessed, having been mortally wounded by a poisoned spear in battle with the Irish, instructs his seven surviving companions to cut off his head and carry it for burial on the White Mount in London, saying that this will act as a wonderful companion to them in their journey, causing them to forget their troubles.

He explains that they will be a long time on the road, spending seven years feasting in Harlech where the birds of Rhiannon will sing to them, and then will reach Grassholm.

They arrive on the island and stay for eighty years, living a life of joy, delight and eternal youth until one of them opens a forbidden door, letting in the sorrows of the past.

They leave to continue their journey and bury the head on the White Mount. The tale ends by relating that no plague will ever come to the island of Britain as long as the head remains concealed in its resting place.

As you round the headland towards Porthlysgi the tower of St Davids Cathedral is visible, a reminder of its proximity to the sea. The beach of Porthlysgi, remote and pebbled at high tide, is named after the Irish chieftain Lysgi who is said to have landed here and slaughtered Boia and his tribe in his hill fort at Clegyr Boia.

Near the stream on the north side of the beach are the remains of the station for St David's first lifeboat, the Augusta. She was launched from here temporarily until the slipway at St Justinians was completed.

Fulmars nest on the tiny island of Carreg Fran, and a mile further on, the harbour of Porthclais suddenly comes into view.

C) From Porthclais Harbour follow the road up the hill to the left of the car park, go straight across at the crossroads following the signposted route to St Justinians.

D) After two hundred yards just to the right on a track below Clegyr Boia follow the footpath immediately left of a bridleway signpost up to the summit. Follow the path down the other side of the hill and turn right along the track, and then right, back onto the road.

For details of Porthclais see page 42. There are stunning views of St Davids and the peninsula from Clegyr Boia. The Boia of legend would have had a very clear sight of the smoke curving above St David's monastic settlement (see page 17).

This volcanic outcrop contains a special piece of prehistory. Sockets ground into the earth around 6,000 years ago to support the timbers of two dwellings, one round and thatched, the other rectangular and timber roofed, were discovered through excavation in the last century; the peninsula's first known farmstead and settlement.

Fragments of Neolithic pottery, a fine stone axe, limpet shells, hearths, a pit for rubbish and the teeth and bones of domesticated oxen make up tantalising fragments in the tale of this family's home and of their means of survival on this windswept plateau of land.

There are no visible traces of the huts, but the site was almost certainly later adapted as an Iron Age hill fort and the now turf-covered defensive walls of this era can be clearly made out, running between the rock outcrops.

E) Turn left at the T-junction, signposted St Justinians, and follow the road back to the lifeboat station.

Wild flowers pattern the roadside edges in vivid clusters of colour, particularly in early summer. To the left is Pwll Trefeiddan, an area of marshland regularly visited by migratory birds and home to a variety of wildfowl.

The late medieval farmhouse of Rhosson Uchaf on the left is one of very few on the peninsula that still retains its so-called Flemish chimney, rising above a huge hearth. Opposite is an old well. Along the road one of the farm outbuildings to the right has small entrances in the west-facing wall for a dovecote. Dovecotes were created for pigeons and doves, which were encouraged to nest as a food source.

As you descend towards St Justinians, the pink tower near the coast is said to have been built as a Victorian folly. The stone in the field opposite the first parking bay is a cattle rubbing stone, as is the one in the field beyond it.

Whitesands Bay

Walks from Whitesands Bay

St Davids Head

This has to be one of the most beautiful coastal walks in Britain, along rugged, dramatic coastline to the stunning headland of the peninsula with its Iron Age fort and views of off-shore islands and a curving Atlantic horizon beyond.

There is ancient farmland with Celtic field patterns almost two thousand years old, a Neolithic burial chamber dating back five thousand years and an optional climb up the granite outcrop of Carn Llidi, an ascent of over 550 feet to one of the most breathtaking views of a coastline you're ever likely to find.

This landscape is so beautiful that, if possible, it is worth walking the area more than once, perhaps varying the route.

Time: Two hours.

Distance: Two miles, with some shorter routes.

Terrain: Moderate walking on the recommended route with some optional, short but steepish, inclines towards the hill of Carn Llidi. The path gets close to the cliff edge in the initial part of this walk.

Facilities: Cafe at Whitesands Bay. WC.

Getting there: From the Cross Square in St Davids take the third exit, as if turning right, carry straight on where the road divides. Take the next left, and left again, following signposts to Whitesands Bay SA62 6PS.

Public transport: The Celtic Coaster.

D
D1
C2
C1
C
Coetan Arthur
Burial Chamber
E
Carnllidi
B
Iron Age
Fort
St Davids Head
Octopitarum
Promontorium
Porth Melgan
Burial Chambers
E1
Porth-mawr
Site of
St Patrick s
Chapel
To St Davids
Whitesands Bay
Whitesands
A
P

Route

A) Take the coast path running north from Whitesands car park. A slight detour left after a few yards will take you to the site of St Patricks Chapel. Continue on the coast path until you near St Davids Head.

At the lowest of tides following a severe winter storm it is possible to come across trunks of trees lying partly submerged in the sand of the beach; a sea-sculpted tumble of oak, birch and hazel over 7,000 years old.

This is a sunken forest of legend and folklore, testament to a time when the sea level was lower and a link, perhaps, with universal tales of flooded lands and lost communities. Such memories live on in this western peninsula.

Tiny, flint spear-points and rare arrowheads discovered amongst these ancient trees and along the present coastline give us tantalising glimpses of the life that the people who lived and survived here at a time when Ramsey Island formed part of a densely wooded mainland.

These finds date from the Mesolithic era, which began at the decline of the last Ice Age 10,000 years ago. The sea level rose, possibly quite suddenly, at around 6,000 BC, to the height it is now, cutting Ramsey Island off from the mainland.

The perfectly preserved jaw of a brown bear and the antlers of an auroch, the fierce, massive ancestor of the European ox, were uncovered in the sand here in the nineteenth century.

The lichen-covered stone inscription at the site of St Patrick's chapel reads, 'Underneath lies a chapel dedicated to St Patrick. Built 6th to 10th century. Excavated 1924.' It is said that St Patrick left for Ireland from Whitesands following a vision in the cathedral valley when an angel showed him the whole of the island of Ireland.

The excavation revealed that the chapel was thirty-four by sixteen feet, with the remains of an altar at the east end and a door in the south wall. The walls, tapering towards the west, were up to three feet thick.

Burials were found, many with offerings of white or quartz stones and limpet shells, which were also found in other areas of the chapel. Many such stones and shells have also been found associated with burials at St Justinians Chapel; white or quartz stones are a feature of many early Celtic Christian burials.

Following erosion of the sand dunes in the severe winter storms of 2013/2014 the site was again excavated in subsequent years. The style of burials suggest that a burial ground was created here in the sixth to the seventh century, with the stone chapel built later and perhaps not going out of use until the sixteenth century.

The storms revealed another auroch antler at Whitesands and the preserved footprint of a mesolithic hunter from 7,000 years ago on nearby Newgale beach.

Hugging the coast near cliff-tops, in the bays, harbours and inlets of the St Davids Peninsula, are many chapel sites of which no visible evidence remains. The two chapels that still exist, at St Nons and St Justinians, are medieval and almost certainly lie on the site of more ancient structures, often known as Celtic sailors' chapels, which were created from the fifth

A Lost Land

The tale of 'Cantre Gwaelod' 'The Lowland Hundred', tells of a great, fertile tract of land that once stretched for over forty miles from the north Pembrokeshire coast across Cardigan Bay.

In the most ancient accounts of the legend, this land was large enough to have contained sixteen splendid townships. It was defended from the rising sea by a series of banks and sluices - defended, that is, until the head keeper of the embankment, a prince named Seithenyn, being worse for wear after a banquet, forgot to order the closure of the sluices. The sea poured through and the land was lost . . .

Some say that on the calmest and clearest of days you can still see the buildings underwater, and, when the sea swell is strong, hear the ringing of church bells.

century onwards in prayer and praise for a voyage's departure or arrival.

They are a reminder of the importance of the sea in the early, missionary days of Celtic Christianity. The peninsula lies at a great intersection point of sea routes linking ancient cultures; a crossroads of travel running south and north, east and west.

In early Christian times there would have been constant passage to and from Ireland and the peninsula through this bay. Whitesands is the nearest crossing point to Ireland, forty-five miles away; in favourable conditions the crossing may have been done in five hours.

The Irish themselves were enthusiastic pilgrims and great travellers. There must have been some who made their prayers here after their arrival, possibly on pilgrimage as far as Spain and Italy. Perhaps some of the limpet shells, a symbol of pilgrimage, found in the chapel were offerings.

Ty Gwyn, the White House, above the beach, is near the site of an early monastery. Tradition has it that St David may have been educated there for a time, becoming leader of the monastery at a young age. The Welsh word, Gwyn, means white, but it can also mean blessed or pure. The most direct gateway into the cathedral close from here is Porth Gwyn, the White Gate.

Whitesands Bay

Further along the coast path to the right you pass the stone walls of what are possibly Iron Age field enclosures, created almost 2,000 years ago. The large boulders above Porth Melgan are known as glacial erratics, carried here from as far as north Wales in the last Ice Age.

As you near St Davids Head the fifteen feet wall of 'The Warrior's Dyke' becomes visible. The two much smaller outer defensive banks of this Iron Age fort and their ditches are just outside this wall. As a defensive settlement it would have been difficult to breach.

The remains of such a high defensive wall are unusual in this area. Smaller ascending banks of stone, now turf-covered, are more common on the coast, but this is a lower promontory than most, yet still formidable.

Passing through the entrance, it is worth pausing and climbing a little higher to your right, from where the foundations of six Iron Age huts are clearly visible, a community dating from around 200 BC.

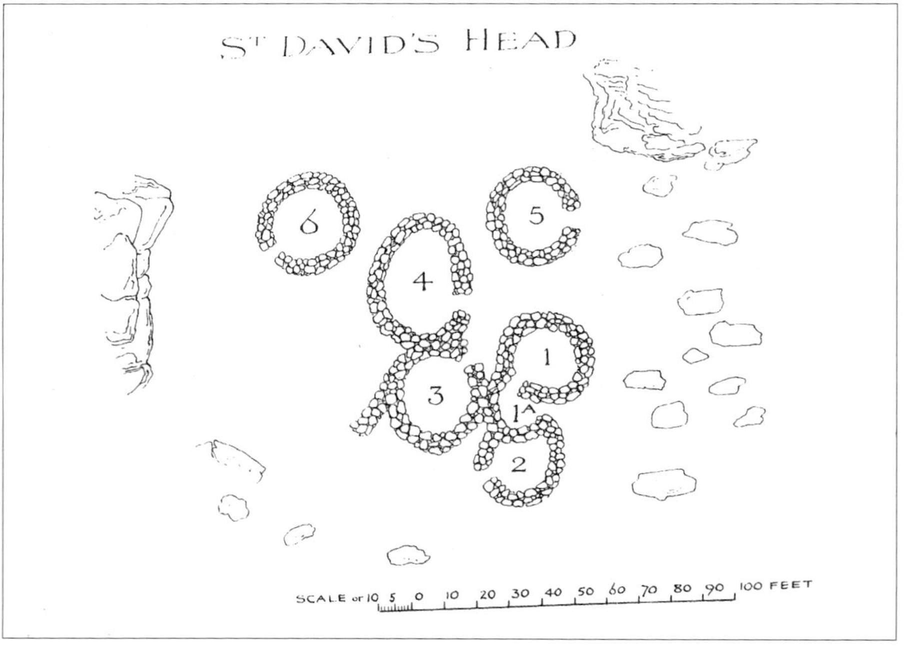

Drawing of the Iron Age hut foundations from the 1898 excavation

Excavation in 1898 revealed that the people living here had some use of iron for implements, and that they practised weaving; intricately decorated spindle whorls were found, along with weights for looms. They also enjoyed decoration; an armlet was discovered, as well as beautiful little perforated purple and blue glass beads. Shards of pottery, possible wheel-made, were also found.

Inland, on the plateau to the north of of Carn Llidi, the stone walls of their field systems can be seen in winter when the bracken is lowest. These field boundaries are at least 2,000 years old and rare in Britain, and are most clearly visible from the slopes of Carn Llidi - appearing mainly as low lines of stones stretching north towards the coast. Some of these boundaries, as on Ramsey Island and Skomer Island to the south, may even date back to the Bronze Age.

Emmer and spelt wheat, barley, beans and peas were widely grown by Iron Age farmers in west Wales, and there would have been some cultivation of crops here. Cattle, pigs, sheep and goats were also reared in the Iron Age. There is a surprising abundance of food in the wild even on this western headland, and the sea and coast would have provided an abundance of fish and shellfish.

Although relatively sheltered from the west and north, and Iron Age huts, snug to the ground with a fireplace in their centre, could be surprisingly warm, it must have been quite a place to live, and almost untenable at times in winter months.[16]

B) There are some lovely places to sit beyond the hut circles before the headland drops down to the sea. From the hut circles take the path to the right towards St Davids Head. Walk back on the same path, keeping to the left. Return through the fort entrance and follow the path to the left onto the higher ground of the ridge and, after four hundred yards just beyond a rocky outcrop, the Neolithic burial chamber of Coetan Arthur will appear on the right.

At St Davids Head the curve of the horizon, and of the earth, is clearly visible. In the second century the Greek geographer Ptolemy, who lived in Roman occupied Alexandria in Egypt, named this headland, Octopitarum Promontorium, the Promontory of the Eight Perils, a reference to the

St Davids Head

islands visible offshore. Vessels of the Roman Empire must have navigated these waters.

In 1603 the historian George Owen wrote that, 'The Bishop and his Clerks', a reference to North Bishop island and the other small islands, 'being seven in number . . . preach deadly doctrine to their winter audience, such poor seafaring men as are forced there by tempest: only in one thing they are to be commended, they keep residence better than the rest of that See are wont to do.'

Porpoises, dolphins and seals can be seen from here and a vast number of seabirds pass this way, including many gannets, cormorants, shags and manx shearwaters. North-west of here is Ireland, look south-west and the nearest landfall is Latin America.

The currents created by the movement of tide can also be seen, flowing clockwise round the head up to high tide, anti-clockwise towards low tide, and stationary for half an hour with each peak of the tide. Seabirds often float on the water around this headland, drifting with the current

Coetan Arthur

of the tide.

Coetan Arthur is a Neolithic burial chamber created around 3,500 BC by the first farmers on the peninsula. This may well have been a place of ancestral worship and of veneration and ritual.

Often referred to in Wales as cromlechs, and older than the pyramids, such chambers bear witness to the birth of an enduring architecture on these shores, and are among the most ancient structures in Britain.

Many interpretations have been made for their spiritual purpose, but what is certain is that they reflect the instincts of their creators.

Survival for these first farmers lay within a turning miracle; in the rise of every sun, in the coming of rain, in the seasonal passage of birth, death and regeneration, in a rhythm of land and sky.

Many scholars suggest that these chambers were created to venerate the seasons and fertility, and that they were possibly womb-like in design, indicating a belief in re-birth.

It is also thought that they were created as a claim to rights to land, rights which were handed down through an ancestral passage of generations; and that many chambers overlook land that would have been cultivated by later generations. Farming and husbandry was often undertaken by people in the presence of their ancestors.

The chambers were communal; there was apparently no hierarchy, no elite. Evidence also indicates that the area before the entrance was a place of ritual and ceremony.

Bones would have been placed in the chambers over many years and may have been brought out and venerated at auspicious times. They were separated and sometimes organised and arranged carefully according to the type of bone.

The angle of the capstone can also appear to emulate that of the hill within sight of them, perhaps this would have been more apparent with the original covering mound - the chambers were originally covered in small stones and turf, generally spreading out two-thirds further than their present extent.

In the creation of the larger chambers, as at Carreg Samson near Trefin, particular care was taken with the choice and siting of types of stone used. The names given to them also suggest the mythic qualities cromlechs have bestowed on the imagination of more recent centuries.

Carn Llidi above Whitesands Bay

It is interesting to speculate that the span of time between the creation of the Iron Age fort on St Davids Head and this burial chamber is greater than that which divides the present time from the Iron Age - were our Celtic forebears as puzzled by these burial chambers as we are now?

So many years after their creation, the Celts are said to have viewed cromlechs as entrances to the Otherworld. They are ancient, compelling architecture.

A local saying tells that if you stay just one night in a cromlech you will either fall in love, become a poet or go mad.

C) From the burial chamber walk north to the coast path. Stay on the coast path until you reach a wall. For a shorter route back, turn right beyond the wall (C1) along a clearly defined path where the path veers to the left or right. There is another short cut along the next clearly defined path to the right near the top of a short incline (C2).

For the recommended route carry straight on along the coast path from the wall until you come to a footpath signpost directing the way to the YHA.

To the right, just behind the wall the foundations of a rectangular and circular hut can be seen. This wall runs from the north coast to near Porth Melgan in the south, and is another mystery. It is built in the classic Iron Age design, integrating stone walls with rock outcrops, but it would have been impossible to defend with the small community on the headland.

It may have began with a larger community in mind, or built as a livestock enclosure for times of impending danger, prior to herding animals into the fort if an attack was imminent.[16] Whatever the reason, it was never completed, as the wall finishes towards the south.

D) Turn right at the YHA sign and follow the path back round, along the valley and back along towards the coast.

The walk along the valley soon becomes really peaceful, with the sound of birdsong and a clear, bubbling stream gathering momentum towards Porth Melgan. There are Iron Age field systems here, and, although they are difficult to make out, the path passes through several low-lying field boundary walls.

To walk up to and around the base of Carn Llidi from (D) *take the next turning left (D1) as you walk towards the valley, this is a steep ascent up some steps. On this route follow the path round the base of the hill, ignoring the first gate to the left. Turn left at the next footpath sign, continue over the stile and follow the track back to Whitesands.*

To ascend Carn Llidi *follow the path until you reach a track on the right going uphill (E1). The track is just to the right of a National Trust sign which is just beyond a gorse bush.*

To ascend Carn Llidi from the route along the valley, *take the wide path to the left on the approach to the coast (E), stay on this path then turn sharp left just after the National Trust sign (E1). Return on the same route, carry straight on past the National Trust sign, take the next right, cross over a stile and follow the lane and road back to Whitesands.*

An alternative route with a slightly gentler incline up towards Carn Llidi is to walk to the coast path, turn left and take the path to the left opposite a large boulder at the top of the hill above Porth Melgan. Turn right when you meet a path going up to Carn Llidi, and follow the directions as at (E1) above.

On the route up Carn Llidi two small Neolithic burial chambers can be seen on the right of the concrete path, just past two metal posts. On the other side of the path, just below a small rocky outcrop, are the remains of a Bronze Age burial cairn. The concrete platform on the lower summit supported a radar station in the Second World War.

A hydrophone, underwater microphone, submarine-listening station was created in the First World War on the western side of the hill, with cables leading down to the coast near Porth Melgan. It is said that this station led to the destruction of up to fifteen German U-boats. Irregular field enclosures can be seen below, denoting their possible Iron Age origin.

Porthselau

Walks from Whitesands Bay

Whitesands and St Justinians

An even walk along a peaceful rural inland path with stunning views of Ramsey Island from the lifeboat station at St Justinians and returning along beautiful coastline, passing the sandy cove of Porthselau. This walk can be muddy in wet weather.

For a lovely family walk with younger children it is possible to take the shorter route, avoiding the busy summer road to St Justinians and some narrow cliff paths. Another good, gentle route with younger children is simply to walk along the coast path to Point St John and back.

Time: Two hours, an hour and a half for the shorter route.

Distance: Two and a half miles, one mile and a half for the shorter route.

Terrain: Easy walking with some short inclines. There is some electric fencing along inland paths. Either route can be muddy in wet weather.

Facilities: Cafe at Whitesands Bay. WC at Whitesands Bay and St Justinians.

Getting there: From the Cross Square in St Davids take the third exit, as if turning right, carry straight on where the road divides. Take the next left, and left again, following signposts to Whitesands Bay SA62 6PS.

Public transport: Celtic Coaster pick-up points at Whitesands and St Justinians.

Coetan Arthur
cromlech
Carnllidi
St Davids Head
Porth Melgan
Site of
St Patricks
Chapel
To St Davids
A
P
Whitesands
Whitesands Bay
Porthselau
Point St John
B1
Upper Treleddyn
B
Pencarnan
St Justinians
Chapel
Rhosson Farm
Clegyr Boia
Ramsey Sound
St Justinians

Route

A) Take the coast path south, past the lifeguard hut, from Whitesands Bay. Take the wide track leading left up a hill opposite Craig-yr-Awel cottage. At the T-junction turn right and follow the track to Treleddyn Farm.

Upper Treleddyn is a substantial eighteenth-century Georgian farmhouse. Local folklore has it is that there was a smugglers' tunnel running from one of the cellars to the cove at Porth Selau.

A heroic rescue of seven shipwrecked mariners was made by Blanch Willias of Upper Treleddyn in 1780, when she spotted men stranded on one of the smaller islands in the group known as the Bishops and Clerks.

Looking towards Carn Llidi

With her husband away, she rowed out single-handed and rescued seven Swedish mariners. Her husband Thomas was the first to give warning of the French invasion of north Pembrokeshire in 1797.

B) For St Justinians turn left along the farm track just after Upper Treleddyn farmhouse. Turn right onto the road at the T-junction, watch out for traffic, then right at St Justinians, following the coast path back to Whitesands.

Details of St Justinians are on page 57. The hedgebanks on this route are a riot of colour in the early summer and the path takes you past the lovely little beach of Porthselau.

B1) For the shorter route, turn right along the signposted footpath just after Upper Treleddyn farmhouse. Follow the path straight ahead and then round to the left at the bottom of the field. Keep children and dogs away from the electric fence on the right along this route.

At the corner of the third field walk over two stiles and down to the beach, the path can be muddy for a short section. It is well worth walking south from here to Point St John before returning along the coast to Whitesands.

Routes to the hill of Carn Llidi

The quickest route if you simply want to get up there, is to walk back up the road from Whitesands and take the second turning left. Walk up the road, then over the stile, after fifty yards turn left and follow the path until you reach a track on the right going uphill. (E1 on the St Davids Head walk map). The track is just to the right of a National Trust sign, which is just beyond a gorse bush.

To return, follow the same path back down, carry straight on past the National Trust sign, take the next right over a stile and follow the lane and road back to Whitesands.

Alternatively there is a beautiful walk that is only slighter longer. At the car park follow the coast path running north. Take the first path to the right after the kissing gate and opposite a large boulder at the top of the hill down to Porth Melgan. Turn right when you meet a path going up to Carn Llidi, then turn sharp left just after the National Trust sign (E1 on the St Davids Head walk map).

Return by the same route, carry straight on past the National Trust sign, take the next right, cross over a stile and follow the lane and road back to Whitesands.

Longer routes from Whitesands Bay

To walk north, follow the coast path to Abereiddy, seven and a half miles, or Porthgain, nine and a half miles, with a fine pub and restaurant. You can make a connection back to St Davids from Abereiddy and Porthgain with the Strumble Shuttle, but, if using public transport, you would need to take the Celtic Coaster from St Davids to Whitesands.

To walk south, follow the coast path to St Justinians, two miles, Porthclais, eight miles, and St Nons, nine miles. You can make a connection back to St Davids from St Justinians and Porthclais on the Celtic Coaster.

Other circular walks on the St Davids Peninsula

Porthgain and Abereiddy

The walk takes in some of the most beautiful areas of the coast path, the haunting beauty of Porthgain with its honeycomb of stone-crushing industrial buildings perched above the harbour's edge, past the wild, remote bay of Traeth Llyfn, to Abereiddy with its slate-tinged sand, the sea-filled quarry of the Blue Lagoon, and ruined cottages, echoing a community's endeavour at the edge of the sea.

Trefin and Abercastle

A walk that follows a wild, beautiful coast curved and shaped into a garland of bays, arches and caves, the evocative remains of a water mill perched above Aberfelin Bay, an Iron Age promontory hill fort and the 4,000 year old burial chamber of Carreg Samson with panoramic views of hills and headlands at the edge of the sea.

The village of Trefin is well worth a visit, with a fine pub and unusual mound of rock at its centre, reflecting a local saying that there are one hundred houses here built on solid rock.

Abermawr Woods

A lovely little walk through woodland and meadows, sheltered from prevailing winds and a riot of bluebells in the spring.

Porthgain

Trefin

Abermawr Woods

Porthgain and Abereiddy

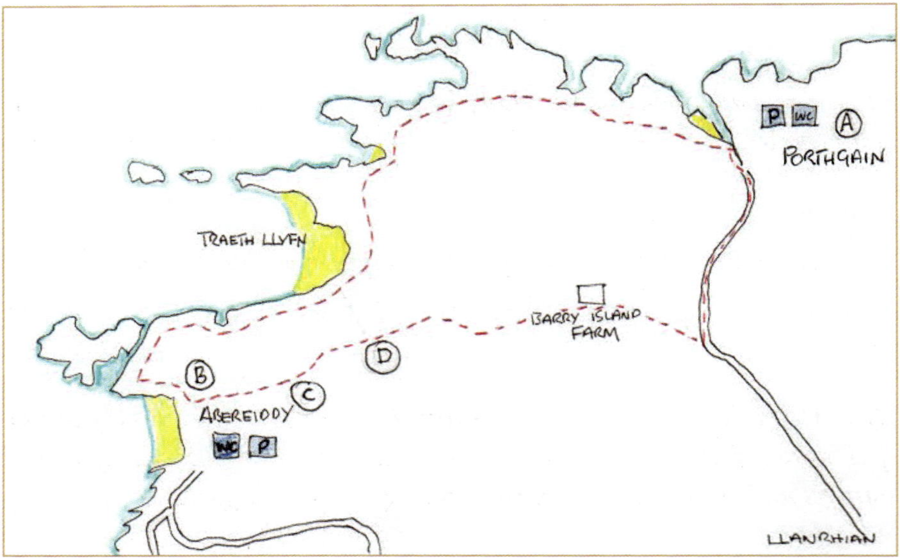

Time: Two hours.

Distance: Three and a half miles.

Terrain: Easy walking along coastline and farmland. Some short inclines. Take care with young children near the steep cliffs at Traethllyfn and Abereiddy; it is possible to route slightly inland at these points.

Facilities: Pub and restaurant,WC in Porthgain. WC at Abereiddy (closed out of season).

487

Getting there: On the A48 St Davids to Fishguard road turn left after six miles at Croesgoch, signposted Porthgain and Llanrhian, straight across at the crossroads and down to Porthgain SA62 5BL.

Public transport: Celtic Coaster pick-up points at Whitesands and St Justinians.

Route

A) From the car park walk to the left around the harbour and up the steps. Follow the coast path to Abereiddy.

B) As you walk towards Abereiddy be aware there are steep cliffs to your right. Walk down towards the bay and turn right along the wide path to visit the Blue Lagoon.

If the ground is wet return along the coast path and turn right inland at the first gate, through the next gate and turn left along the farm track at (D).

C) For the inland walk from Abereiddy – there is one short muddy section if the ground is wet - at the car park turn left past the row of ruined cottages and the public convenience, then go through a gate.

Follow the path uphill for 50 yards then turn right along the former tramway track leading inland above the valley. Go through the next stile and follow the path along the right side of the field.

D) Turn right along the farm track at the next stile. Follow the track through the farm and left at the T-junction and down the road to Porthgain. Stay left on the road as there are some concealed bends.

To return by the coast from here (D) cross the next gate opposite you. straight ahead to the next gate and on to the coast path.

Trefin and Abercastle

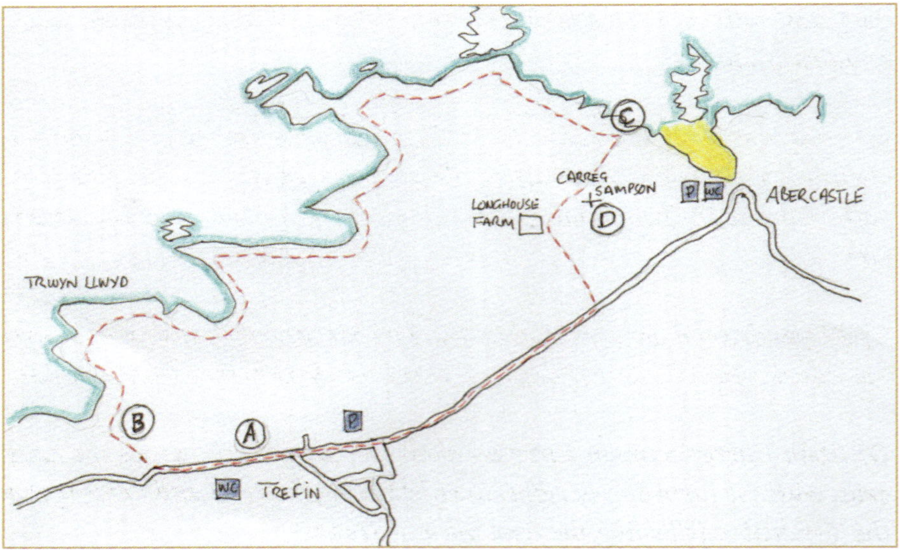

Time: Two and a half hours

Distance: Three and a half miles

Terrain: Easy walking along coastline and farmland, but the route is not suitable for dogs or young children as there is a section of steep cliffs. Some short inclines at the start of the walk. The return is a twenty minute walk along a country road.

Facilities: A pub and cafe in Trefin. WC (open in summer) below the Ship Inn.

Getting there: From the A48 St Davids to Fishguard road, turn left after seven miles, signposted Trefin SA62 5AL. Turn left into the village and park in the main street. There is limited parking just above the mill at the bottom of the hill.

Public transport: Strumble Shuttle and Richards Brothers bus service.

Route

A) Descend the hill past the Ship Inn and, after the road bears left, take the grass path on the right just after a telegraph pole and down to the remains of the mill.

B) From the mill turn right along the coast path and past the ruins of quarried stone working buildings. There are steep cliffs as you follow the path round to the headland of Pen Castell-coch, an Iron Age promontory fort.

C) As you descend towards Abercastle Harbour take the turning right over the stile signposted 'Carreg Samson' to the burial chamber (See page 50)

D) From Carreg Samson carry up along the farm track, across the cattle grids with the farm on you right. Bear left along the road and turn right at the T-junction following the road back to Trefin.

Abermawr Woods

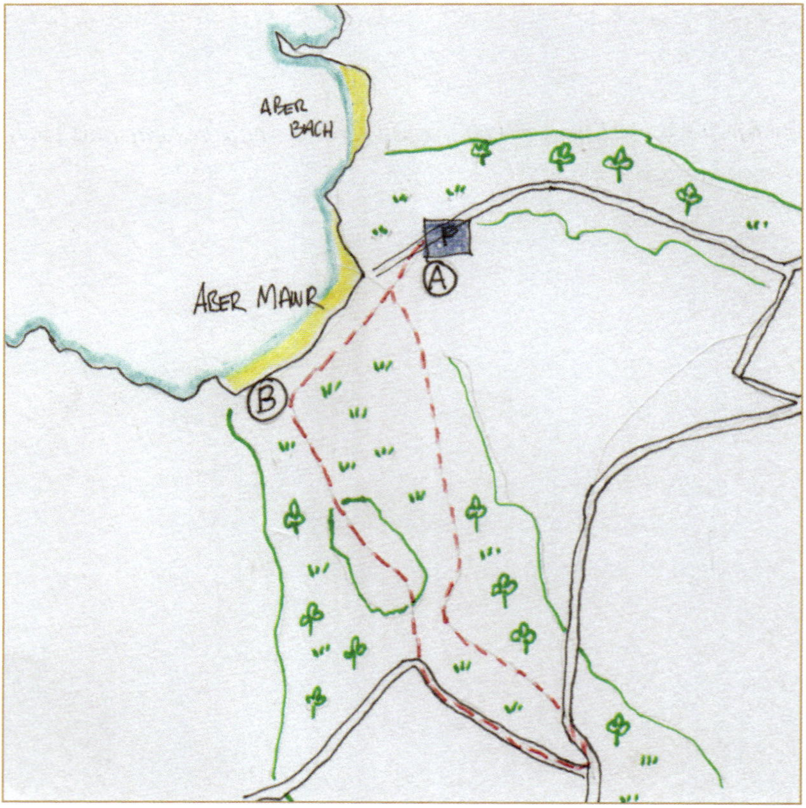

Time: One hour

Distance: Two miles

Terrain: Easy walking along coastline and woodland paths.

Facilities: Cafe and WC at nearby Tregwynt Woolen Mill.

Getting there: From the A48 St Davids to Fishguard road, turn left after nine miles, signposted Abermawr and Tregwynt Woolen Mill. Follow signs to Abermawr. Roadside parking, limited in the summer.

Public transport: None

Route

A) Walk along the beach and take the path (B) into the woods at the south end of the beach.

Follow the path until you reach a gate with a road beyond and turn left back into the woods and to the beach.

Bibliography

Archaeolgia Cambrensis 5th series, vol XVI.

Bowen E.G. The St David of History. Cambrian News. 1982.

Browne L. Willis. Survey of the Cathedral Church of St Davids. 1717.

Cambrensis G. The Itinerary through Wales and the Description of Wales. Penguin. 1978.

Chadwick N. The Celts. Penguin Books. 1970

Charles B. G. The Place-Names of Pembrokeshire. National Library of Wales. 1982.

Davies P. B. S. The Footsteps of our Fathers. Merrivale. 1994.

Davies P. B. S. Forgotten Mines. Merrivale. 1990.

Evans W. and Roger Worsley. St Davids Cathedral. Yr Oriel Fach. 1981.

Evans W. St Davids Cathedral. Pitkin Guides. 1991.

Evans W. and Turner R. eds. St David of Wales: Cult, Church and Nation. Boydell. 2007.

Evans D. The Welsh Life of St David. University of Wales. 1988.

Evans H. Twr-y-Felin History and Guide to St Davids. Menpes Printing. 1923.

Fenton R. A. A Historical Tour through Pembrokeshire. Dyfed County Council. 1994

George B. Pembrokeshire Sea Trade before 1900. Headley Bros. 1965.

Gray M. The Pre-Christian Origins of European Pilgrimage. Internet site. 2012.

Howells R. The Sounds Between. Llandysul Gomerian. 1968.

Hampson D. and Middleton G. The Story of the St Davids Lifeboats. Five Arches. 1989.

James D.W. St Davids and Dewisland, A Social History. University of Wales. 1981.

James D. W. Twice to St Davids. Gomer. 1995.

James H and James T. Ramsey Island Prehistoric Field System. Archaeology in Wales. 1994.

John T. and Rees N. Pilgrimage, A Welsh Perspective. Gomer. 2002.

Jones F. The Holy Wells of Wales. University of Wales. 1954.

Jones W. B. and Freeman E. A. History and Antiquities of St Davids. Pembrokeshire Council Cultural Services. 1998.

Kilvert. F. Kilvert's Diary 1870-1879. Penguin. 1999.

Middleton G. The Streets of St Davids. Yr Oriel Fach. 1977.

Owen G. Description of Pembrokeshire, ed. Dillwyn Miles. Gomer Press. 1998.

Rees N. St David of Dewisland. Gomer Press. 2008.

Wade-Evans A. W. Life of St David. Society for Promoting Christian Knowledge. 1923.

Willis-Bund, J W (ed.) The Black Book of St Davids. London. 1902.

Notes

1. James D. W. Twice to St Davids. Gomer Press. 1995.
2. James D.W. St Davids and Dewisland, A Social History. University of Wales. 1981
3. Evans H. Twr-y-Felin History and Guide to St Davids. 1923.
4. Evans W. St Davids Cathedral. Pitkin Guides. 1991; Charles B. G. The Place-Names of Pembrokeshire. National Library of Wales. 1982; Wade-Evans A. W. Life of St David. Society for Promoting Christian Knowledge. 1923.
5. Gray M. The Pre-Christian Origins of European Pilgrimage. Internet site. 2012.
6. Jones F. The Holy Wells of Wales. University of Wales. 1954.
7. John T. and Rees N. Pilgrimage, A Welsh Perspective. Gomer. 2012.
8. Jones F. The Holy Wells of Wales. University of Wales. 1954.
9. Jones F. The Holy Wells of Wales. University of Wales.1954.
10. Charles B. G. The Place-Names of Pembrokeshire. National Library of Wales. 1982.
11. George B. Pembrokeshire Sea Trade before 1900. Headley Bros. 1965.
12. James D.W. St Davids and Dewisland, A Social History. University of Wales. 1981.
13. Hampson D. and Middleton G. The Story of the St Davids Lifeboats. Five Arches. 1989.
14. James D.W. St Davids and Dewisland, A Social History. University of Wales. 1981.
15. Jones F. The Holy Wells of Wales. University of Wales. 1954.
16. Rev. Baring-Gould. Exploration of the Stone Camp on St Davids Head. Archaeolgia Cambrensis 5th series, vol XVI.

With grateful thanks to Julie Trier for invaluable editorial advice, Grahame Hurd-Wood for the oil paintings and Terry James for the line drawings.

Grahame Hurd-Wood:
www.newstreetgallerystdavids.wordpress.com

St Nons Lane

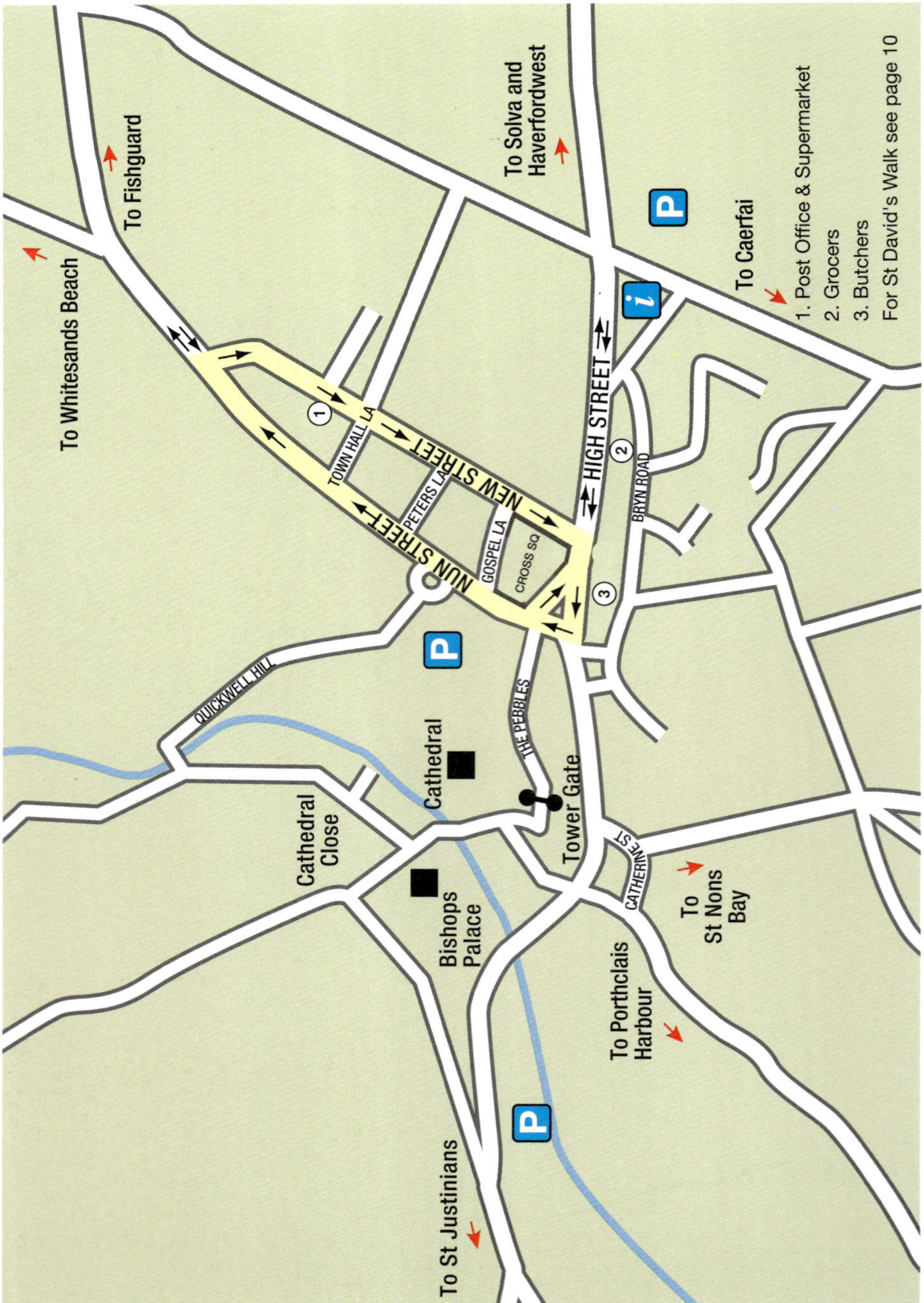

To Whitesands Beach
To Fishguard
To Solva and Haverfordwest
To Caerfai
TOWN HALL LA
NEW STREET
HIGH STREET
PETERS LA
GOSPEL LA
CROSS SQ
NUN STREET
BRYN ROAD
QUICKWELL HILL
THE PEBBLES
Cathedral
Cathedral Close
Tower Gate
Bishops Palace
CATHERINE ST
To St Nons Bay
To Porthclais Harbour
To St Justinians
1. Post Office & Supermarket
2. Grocers
3. Butchers
For St David's Walk see page 10